EMPLOYER'S GUIDE
TO HIRING
AND FIRING

Paul Preston, Ph.D., a management professor at the University of Texas at San Antonio, is a consultant specializing in conflict management, personnel problems, performance appraisal, communication, and time management. He has written several articles and books on management, including *Communication for Managers, Management for Supervisors, Business: An Introduction to American Enterprise,* and *Student Guide to Business,* all published by Prentice-Hall.

Prentice-Hall, Inc., Englewood Cliffs, New Jersey 07632 A SPECTRUM BOOK

PAUL PRESTON

Strategies, Tactics,
and Legal Considerations

EMPLOYER'S GUIDE
TO HIRING
AND FIRING

Library of Congress Cataloging in Publication Data

Preston, Paul (date)
    Employer's guide to hiring and firing.

    "A Spectrum Book."
    "Includes index.
    1. Recruiting of employees.   2. Employees, Dismissal of.
I. Title.
HF5549.5.R44P73   1982   658.3′112   82-7651
ISBN 0-13-274571-2   AACR2
ISBN 0-13-274563-1 (pbk.)

This Spectrum Book can be made available to businesses
and organizations at a special discount when ordered in
large quantities. For more information, contact:
Prentice-Hall, Inc., General Publishing Division,
Special Sales, Englewood Cliffs, New Jersey 07632.

1   2   3   4   5   6   7   8   9   10

ISBN 0-13-274571-2

ISBN 0-13-274563-1 {PBK.}

Editorial/production supervision by Maxine Bartow
Cover design by Jeannette Jacobs
Calligraphy by Michael Freeland
Manufacturing buyer: Barbara A. Frick

Prentice-Hall International, Inc., London
Prentice-Hall of Australia Pty. Limited, Sydney
Prentice-Hall Canada Inc., Toronto
Prentice-Hall of India Private Limited, New Delhi
Prentice-Hall of Japan, Inc., Tokyo
Prentice-Hall of Southeast Asia Pte. Ltd., Singapore
Whitehall Books Limited, Wellington, New Zealand

This book is dedicated to
Kimberly Noël Preston
with love

Contents

This book is for the manager or supervisor who is facing three of the most difficult problems it is possible to face in this profession: hiring the right people, counseling and disciplining people when their performance becomes a problem, and firing them when circumstances warrant.

In most business schools and in most supervisory training programs these topics are given little or no attention. Instead, there tends to be a focus on such important topics as planning, controlling, organizing, and motivating. There is little doubt that these, and other important topics, are vital for effective supervision; however, they are not the topics that cause supervisors the most concern.

In a recent survey of participants in a seminar for Newly Appointed Supervisors, I had the occasion to ask the group what problems they feared most as they looked forward to the challenges of their new jobs. The response was revealing. Forty percent cited having to deal with problem employees—those who can be salvaged but whose behavior must be changed if they are to continue in the department or section; another 30 percent cited interviewing and hiring new people, especially when their success as a supervisor depended on getting and keeping good employees. The final 30 percent feared having to fire an employee, either for just cause or because of circumstances beyond anyone's direct control.

Thinking these results were because of the inexperience and lack of self-confidence one would expect of new supervisors, I tried the same question with more experienced supervisors in a variety of organizations. Surprisingly, the proportions citing hiring, counseling, and firing when asked "what parts of your job do you feel least pre-

Preface

pared to handle?'' were the same as those of the new supervisor group. Obviously, I thought, there is a real problem that is not being addressed by the current materials available to supervisors.

This book is the result of the research that began with those questions.

Most of the strategies included in this book have been suggested by managers who have been successful in hiring, counseling, or firing. Keep in mind that personal supervisory style plays a big part in any approach to a thorny problem. Some of the tactics cited in this book will require some personal modification before they'll prove useful to you. Others can be used "right off the shelf." But there was one common thread that ran through all the suggestions and contributions from the managers surveyed in preparing this book: when in doubt, ask someone who knows, someone who has been there. In some cases, you'll want to consult with your firm's legal counsel. In other cases, an experienced manager or a person from the personnel office or labor relations staff will be your best source of help.

There are five major sections in this book. The major sections are those that deal directly with hiring, counseling, and firing. As we note in Chapter 1, some of the material in one section (for example, firing) might be unnecessary if you did the proper things when dealing with the counseling problems earlier in the situation. And counseling may not have been necessary if you'd done a better job of hiring in the first place. Thus, some of the information may be unnecessary. However, read it all, and store away for future use those strategies, tactics, and approaches that especially appeal to you. When problems erupt, there is rarely enough time for you to go to your bookshelves for advice. These days, preparation is the mark of the effective manager.

Part of your overall preparation for the problems discussed between these covers is contained in Chapter 1, Chapter 14, and the Appendix.

Chapter 1 asks you to do a bit of self-analysis. Examine carefully your strengths, weaknesses, biases, and predispositions. Change those that you think need changing. Keep those that you find profitable. Above all, know yourself before you tackle any of these challenges.

Chapter 14 addresses an all-too-prevalent problem for managers and supervisors today—that of stress. We are increasingly subject to the damaging effects of stress, from a variety of causes and sources. Ordinary job pressures, family pressures, inflation, world politics, congestion, and general uncertainty all combine to create severe pressures on us even in the best of times. When additional burdens are placed on us through the need to hire, counsel, or fire employees, the burden can become too much. Damaging stress and its physical, mental, and emotional side effects are not far behind. Chapter 14 contains both mental and physical approaches to reducing stress to manageable levels.

Although the Appendix may seem unusual for a book on hiring, counseling, and firing, it is designed to give you some feeling for the kind of advice job applicants are regularly given when they prepare resumes. The hiring phase of this book is the only one where the raw material comes from outside our organizations. We produce our own problem employees and firing cases, but in hiring, we take what comes in. Therefore, it is often important for us to know a little about how these unknown persons are preparing for their interaction with us. This Appendix, Writing a Professional Resume, appeared first in *Association Management*, a publication for persons who manage trade and professional associations. The advice in it is similar to advice given to applicants in every college, university, secondary school, and "self-help" publication. Read it carefully, and you'll know a little more about how your prospective employees are preparing for *their* interviewing challenge.

Book writing does not take place in a vacuum. This book is the result of a group effort, for which I get to take primary credit as the author. However, it is because of the interest, care, and contribution of a great many people that it came to be.

I would like to thank the editors and authors who permitted me to use their materials in this book. Among them are Peter Patau, Debra J. Stratton, Dr. John Burns, and many others.

Joyce C. Ronemous deserves a special note of thanks for her work researching the legal aspects of firing.

Many other people contributed their ideas and their support. Dean E. Douglas Hodo and Dr. William D. Litzinger of the College of Business, University of Texas at San Antonio, provided support and encouragement. So did Paul Halliday, Kathryn Barber, and Ingrid Norrish at Humber College in Toronto, Canada; General William Lindley, Catherine Haydn, and Joan Nitschke of the University of Texas at San Antonio, Division of Continuing Education; Peggy Dame, R.N., at the University of Texas Nursing School in San Antonio; Joyce Hoover, R.N., at the University of Texas Nursing School in Austin; and Dr. Barbara Hauf at the University of North Dakota School of Nursing.

Other friends who offered their suggestions and comments at various phases of this project include Terry Townsend, Texas Motor Transportation Association; Ron Galbraith and James Pilversack of the Hospital Corporation of America; Sr. Irene Kraus of Providence Hospital, Washington, D.C.; O. Ray Hurst and Joe DaSilva of the Texas Hospital Association; Peggy McCollum of McCollum Meetings &

Management; Jim Ritchie of the Alabama Trucking Association; Jayne Seigal of La Quinta Motor Inns, Inc.; Dr. Thomas Atchison of the American College of Hospital Administrators; William J. Durbin of the Carrier Corporation; Jim Jenkins of Sigmor Industrial Lubricants Co.; Frank D. Haegelin, City Public Service Company of San Antonio; Carolyn Loftis of Rauscher Pierce Refsnes, Inc.; Larry Pitcaithly of Schlumberger Well Service, Inc.; Marilyn Monroe of the Texas Society of Association Executives; and Charles and Kay Knapp of the Food Industry Association Executives. There are countless others who have also contributed to this work.

A special thanks to my coauthors on many of the materials that appear in this book by way of earlier incarnations in professional journals: Brian Hawkins, Thomas Rohan, Harry David, Tom Zimmerer, Bill Mitchell, Lou Seiberlich, Anthony Quesada, and Phil Johnson. Another thanks to Jean Bolton and Bobbie Roberts for their help.

With support such as I've cited above, there can't be many errors. If there are any, I am responsible.

Hundreds of men and women have participated over the past few years in seminars and programs of Preston Associates, Inc. Their questions started this book on the long road to your hands, and their contributions give this book both its practical outlook and pragmatic tone. To all of them, and to you for reading this book, thank you.

1
Introduction

Welcome to the ins and outs of management. This book is designed to take you, the manager, through some of the most difficult stages in your professional life: the hiring of effective employees, the counseling of problem employees, and the firing of those people who for one reason or another can no longer remain employees of the organization.

All of these problems present challenges. Indeed, the top management of many an organization consider these three areas to be the most crucial of any manager's career. These organizations watch how managers hire, counsel, and fire employees, using an individual's performance as a guide to later career moves. In short, your own chances for being hired for future promotion will depend on how you hire others to work for you. Your ability to move up the organization chart will be directly linked to how well you manage those under your command. And your tenure or longevity with an organization will depend on your ability to get rid of those persons who are no longer productive for the organization.

Management, as taught in schools, usually is described as having four functions. We are taught that managers spend their days planning, organizing, directing, and controlling, and that all managerial activity relates in some way to one or more of these important functions. However, the illusion that *all* managers do is plan, organize, direct, and control masks the fact that much of the manager's real day-to-day activity is wound up in "people problems." People do not work for an organization until they are hired. They do not produce for the organization unless they are told what to do and what not to do in a way that causes them to do what they are supposed to do. And they keep the organization from reaching its goals when they remain employed by the organization beyond the time when their contributions are required. In short, the four functions of management might be rewritten as the three challenges of management: *hiring, counseling, and firing.*

HIRING

In some organizations, only certain managers have any control over who is hired, and on what terms. Other managers are simply given a number of employees and told to organize and manage those employees to reach certain results; these managers have no choice in the matters of hiring. In other organizations, managers at all levels have virtually total control over who is hired, and they dictate the terms of employment as well. The common practice is somewhere in between, although such things as organizational level also play a part. For example, in one organization, managers who work with operating (or nonmanagerial) employees, are given a "pool" of persons qualified for a particular position. The manager can choose whichever prospective employees she wishes. Someone else (usually a personnel department) has screened the applicants to determine which ones have the necessary skills and otherwise meet the organization's minimum qualifications for the job. In that same organization, the persons in higher management have considerable control over who works for them, although they are bound by the organization's hiring policies. One of those policies requires that all presently employed persons who meet the qualifications for a managerial job opening must be given preference over outsiders. Another policy is that a manager's choice of subordinates must be approved by the manager's immediate superior. Still another policy is that managers must consult with other managers before bringing outsiders into the firm. Thus, although an individual manager may have more direct control over who is employed, she must still share the responsibility for making the proper choice of a new employee for her department.

In many cases, a person coming into an organization is given almost a free hand in hiring subordinates. This woman or man may bring in anyone she or he feels can do the job required, subject only to that person meeting certain minimum qualifications. For example, if a defense contractor wanted to bring in certain persons as managers, each of the prospective managers would have to be able to pass a government security check required of all the firm's employees. In companies with a rule against nepotism (employing relatives of persons already employed by the firm), a prospective employee would be required to attest that he is not related to any present employees. Of course, other bona fide qualifications relating to a specific job would also have to be considered.

The importance of the hiring responsibility on a manager's own career is considerable. When we elect a new president, we expect him to bring into the government at the top levels the best men and women available. The citizens expect that their government will be run with efficiency, style, compassion, and effectiveness, and we look to the president's top appointees to deliver on both his promises and our expectations. Consider the number of past U.S. presidents who have found themselves in trouble with the voters over the apparently poor choices they made in hiring their immediate subordinates. These days, one can almost pick up a newspaper any day of the week and find another example of poor hiring leading to a politician getting into hot water with the voters. In business organizations, the same thing happens all the time. The quality of a particular manager, as well as his real worth to the company in the future, is often determined by how well (or poorly) he hires. Making a wise choice when hiring can bathe a manager in continuing good will from above. Making a poor choice, and then dealing poorly with the choice, can be an unending source of embarrassment and ill will and can ultimately lead to the hirer's downfall.

One often-cited definition of effective management is "the ability to find and hire the best people, and then get out of their way and let them produce . . . while you sit back and take the credit."

It's probably not that simple, but effective hiring is essential, both to the organization's survival and profitability and to the manager's career success.

COUNSELING

Hiring and firing are specific topics. They deal with events that occur at a certain time in an employee's life with an organization. Most managers know when they are supposed to be hiring—or firing—and they can prepare for the "chore" or the "challenge." Counseling is more difficult to define because it happens over a longer period of time and is conducted in a number of different ways and settings. If "directing" is one of the four functions of management, counseling is the part of directing that is aimed at those employees who require more directing than others. This may include employees who need more training, closer supervision, or more detailed instructions to do their jobs. It may also include those employees who know what they are supposed to do, but for any number of reasons are either unable or unwilling to do what is expected of them. These are the problem employees, prime candidates for firing if their behavior and their performance do not change for the better.

Rather than counseling, some managers prefer to think of this challenge as "salvaging." They contend, with considerable justification, that the manager who is held accountable for her hiring decisions and for effective work performance *must* salvage those who are doing unacceptable work. To these managers, firing is not an option. They feel that if too many people are fired, top management will become suspicious of the management ability of the firer. Also, firing employees who do not perform up to expectations can be costly to the company. Each person hired and then fired means that another person must be screened, hired, and trained in his place. Many people, faced with high new car prices, decide to fix up their old cars and drive them a little while longer. They know that eventually they may have to replace their old cars, but at least they can get a few more miles out of them first. This is the same dilemma facing managers: Do I replace my troublesome employee or find a replacement? Which course will be less costly? More profitable? Which course of action will make me look best (or keep me from looking bad) in the eyes of my management? How can I make the best of a bad situation or keep a bad situation from getting worse?

If the manager's decision in the salvage-or-discharge situation is salvage, how can it be done? How can he change problem or unproductive behavior into productive or proper behavior?

The first step is to develop a better understanding of the problem employee, why he has become a problem, and why he behaves the way we now label "a problem." We must also know what constitutes correct, profitable, or proper behavior for that employee. It does little good to tell an employee that he is doing wrong if we cannot tell him what is right. Thus, some self-analysis and job performance analysis are necessary.

Behavior change comes about as a result of persuasion and of desire on the part of the individual to change. Changing problem behavior requires motivation, not authority or legislation. Motivation means learning how to communicate with the problem employee, how to point out the problem behavior without provoking defensiveness, how to communicate the desired behavior, and how to create in the employee a feeling that behaving properly will result in benefits to him.

Salvaging problem employees also means working out day-to-day problems and conflicts before they reach the stage where problem behavior exists. Minor problems, if not handled properly, can result in even the most dedicated or productive employee's behavior turning unproductive. We may create some of our problem behaviors for ourselves, by not properly managing conflict when it occurs. Creative conflict management is thus an essential part of any manager's repertory of counseling skills.

FIRING

How often do managers actually fire employees? According to statistics available, the answer is very rarely. People do leave organizations involuntarily, but it is difficult to tell exactly how many. The statistics are clouded by the many euphemisms we use to avoid saying "fired."

Firing is a fact of organizational life. Everyone who hires on with a firm cannot expect to remain employed as long as she wishes. For any number of reasons, some within the control of the individual employee, some beyond her control, some of those presently working will have their employment terminated. They will be fired.

Firing is perhaps the most distasteful task facing any manager. Many managers, through luck and skill at organizational maneuvering, go through an entire career, with one or many organizations, without having to fire anyone. Other managers find themselves constantly coming up on the "fire" end of the salvage-or-discharge decision.

Just as there are different managerial experiences with firing, there are many styles and approaches to doing the firing. Some of these approaches amount to running away from the problem, avoiding the responsibility in favor of hoping that the offending employee will get the message and resign. Other firing approaches resemble medieval executions in their subtlety and compassion. There is no right way to fire, but most managers know a variety of ways *not* to fire. The only trouble is that, when faced with having to fire someone, these same managers revert to the old and unproductive methods. There has to be a better way.

Complicating the firing picture is the fact that in difficult economic times it becomes necessary to fire employees who do not deserve to be fired. Mergers, reorganizations, changes in corporate strategy, along with declining or changing markets, result in persons who have been doing productive work being terminated. Handling these people—while remaining mindful of the effect of the firings on the remaining employees—requires considerable skill, tact, and compassion. The "meat-axe" approach to firing, ineffective when a firing is deserved, becomes downright dangerous to an organization's continued survival and profitability when used on those who do not deserve to lose their jobs.

Another consideration in firing is the effect a person's firing ability can have on his own career. Just as good hiring can lead to career opportunities and promotions, firing can be beneficial to one's future prospects. Firing is so distasteful to so many managers in so many organizations that those managers who do fire well become superstars. They develop a reputation that may result in their being given assignments involving firing just because no one else will do it or do it so well. Each time a manager who fires well helps out a fellow manager by relieving her of the burden, the firer gains an ally in the corporate wars. Effectively firing others has been the route to the top for a significant number of today's top managers who now expect firing skill from their subordinates as a ticket to the top.

Apart from considerations that begin to sound Machiavellian, effective firing can be viewed as another of any manager's talents. Taken by itself, firing can take on an almost mystical aura. It seems to embody all that is supposedly wrong with management and wrong with organizations, as well. Viewed as one part of the management process, as important as planning, organizing, directing, and controlling, its real value becomes clearer.

ONE BEST WAY?

Managers seem to be constantly on a search for the one best way to perform any of their managerial responsibilities. Yet, just as surely as there is no one best way to lead, motivate, organize, or plan, there is no one best way to inverview, hire, counsel, persuade, or fire. Each situation must be taken by itself. Each set of circumstances will determine which skills and subtle nuances of the manager's art will be appropriate at that time. To assume any constant or set schedule is to invite failure. The topics in this book and the discussion of those topics were chosen because they cover some of the basics. They do not purport to be the one best way.

SELF-ANALYSIS

In all three areas of this book, we confront a reality. How we hire (counsel, fire) is a reflection of ourselves. We often try to hire those who remind us of our most desirable qualities (whether we actually possess those qualities or not). In counseling problem employees, we usually counsel the way we have been counseled—which too often means poorly. When we fire, we rely on our limited experience, either of being fired (which happens to very few of us) or of the stories we've heard from or about those who have been fired.

To be effective in the skills this book addresses, we must first look at the people perfecting and using those skills—ourselves. Ask yourself the following simple questions and consider some of the issues and answers below each question. The viewpoints raised will be discussed throughout the balance of this book. Be honest, and look for potential strengths as well as weaknesses.

Can You Objectively Evaluate Yourself?   Strange as it may seem, the same managers who are capable and self-assured when evaluating the performance of their employees are often unable to turn the mirror on themselves.[1] In particular, they are able to identify their own weaknesses, but they come up short when forced to list or identify their strengths. Despite the fact that most managers usually have positive self-images, they often have difficulty being objective. Others may not see you in the same light that you shine on yourself, but that is no reason to shrink from making an objective assessment.

How Do You Take Bad News?   Do you react poorly when a member of your staff brings you information that's bad? Does your response to bad news ever take the form of accusing the bad-news bearer of being the cause of the bad news? Does your facial expression suggest (even if your voice doesn't) that you are holding the news bearer personally responsible?

Managers who are good at handling bad news are fully aware of the impact nonverbal (or body) messages can have, especially in pressure- or anxiety-producing situations. They know too that the surest way to eliminate bad news is to make people feel you don't want any bad news. Of course, this doesn't make the bad news go away. It's still there waiting to jump out at you when you're not expecting it. As a manager of a department or organization, you like to receive good news. You like to hear that sales are up, the quality index averages are rising, employee turnover is down, and employees are contented and productive. Although good news is nice to have, managers must realize that it's the bad news they need to do the job they are supposed to do. Without bad news to handle, there would be little reason for your job in the organization. Cutting off your sources of vital information is foolhardy. If you're guilty of this, consider the following ideas:

Good bad-news takers learn to delay their reactions to information, whether delivered orally or in writing. Since first reactions are usually impulsive, they don't reflect your true feeling anyway. They can usually cause only harm. Also, reinforce people who bring you bad news by showing in some way that you appreciated their prompt report. And if the person who brings you bad news is the one responsible for the bad news, delayed reaction is still good advice. Assuming that people learn from their errors, a delayed reaction can help maintain an open line of communication for the next time the culprit brings you his tale of woe.

Do You Learn from Your Mistakes, or Do You Constantly Reinvent the Wheel?   Practically perfect people rarely make mistakes, but few managers are perfect. Therefore, when mistakes happen, you have two choices. You can admit nothing, blame it on poor staff work, and risk the same thing happening again.

Or, you can admit error, take realistic stock of causes and implications, and make changes to avoid a recurrence. Managerial effectiveness is judged on one's ratio of good-to-bad decisions, not on some absolute standard of perfection. You improve your "win-lose" record when you plan ahead and foresee potential errors and problems. Failure to honestly appraise errors (especially your own) also deprives you of information that can make the next similar error easier to handle. Without this "experimental information," each new outcropping of an old problem becomes a novel situation. In effect, you must reinvent the wheel for each trip, instead of building on the performance and experience of the past.

Can You Listen to Others and Learn from Them?   Listening is a skill we often take for granted. We confuse listening and hearing, which is a physical process. In contrast, listening involves understanding and evaluating what others say—making their input a part of your frame of reference. If you find your attention wandering as you listen to others, or if you are thinking about your next comment instead of concentrating on what the other person is saying, you may have a listening handicap.

Overcoming listening problems requires a change in your personal way of communicating with people. Become person oriented. Try to understand not just what a person says, but also why he says it. Assume when you're listening that you are responsible for both ends of the message (sender and receiver) and not just your part. You'll develop what experts call active listening skills.

Can You Filter out Unnecessary Information?   Although listening skills are essential to good management, too much information can be dangerous. Individuals who are unable to decide between the relevant and irrelevant information coming at them from all directions run the risk of "information overload." In its extreme form, it can result in an inability to function as a manager. There is simply too much data for a person to find the *necessary* data, and the end result is almost the same as a complete absence of information.

For most managers, information overload is not quite so serious. Its usual symptoms are a feeling that there's never enough time to get everything done. The manager feels pressured. He seems to be searching for more data, even though there's perhaps too much data available already.

There are three common cures for information overload. Two of them (delegation and better decision making) will be discussed below. A third strategy is to develop mental filters capable of sorting out the wheat from the chaff. This can be done by assigning priorities to various kinds of inputs and then staying with your priorities. It can be done by attaching a time frame to everything you hear. For example, if you're told that the loan committee has a policy statement prepared, evaluate whether this information should be handled immediately or if it can be temporarily ignored. If it can wait, put it aside and keep it from cluttering up your "handle immediately" information.

A credit union supervisor in Nebraska suggests that his "filter" is to preface every piece of data he receives with the question "will it be important six months from now?" If the answer is no, he ignores the information, putting it aside until he has otherwise free time. Perhaps your "time horizon" is one year, or one week. Nevertheless, such devices can help you avoid overload problems.

Can You Delegate, or Must You Take Personal Charge of All Activities?   Failure to delegate can often be a manager's sign of lack of trust in her subordinates. It can also indicate a personal insecurity that is both counterproductive and time-consuming. The result of a failure to delegate can often be the information overload to which we referred above.

Improving your delegation skill might involve better training for the people on your staff. It may mean breaking what has been called the "low-trust low-performance" cycle. Low management trust (such as a failure to delegate) leads to employees' performance slipping. This in turn leads to a further erosion of your trust in them. To break the cycle, managers must take a crucial first step and give employees responsibility in situations where perhaps they haven't earned such responsibility. This step won't always work, but it does work often enough to suggest that it is possible to improve one's skill at delegation.

How Do You Handle Crisis?   Times of crisis can be revealing. They may show us some things about ourselves that may not be altogether complimentary, or they may show us hidden strengths and abilities we did not know we possessed.

The cool performance of professionals in crisis situations is often revealing. It suggests that crisis can be managed if we develop the appropriate attitude toward it. Recall the moon landings of a few years ago. We all remember the brave crew of *Apollo 8*, the first to circle the moon on Christmas Eve, 1968. We remember Armstrong, Aldrin, and Collins of *Apollo 11*. In time, moon landings became routine. We knew the astronauts would get home safely, even if their luggage didn't. Things were so routine for civilians and crews alike that we assumed if an engine blew up in flight, the crew might respond, "Did you feel that? Pass the Tang." Yet when just such a crisis developed on *Apollo 13,* they *were* prepared. When a vital system did explode, Jim Lovell's first words to NASA base were, "Houston, I think we have a problem." No panic. No surprise. No blame. He and his colleagues were in charge. They managed their crisis and came through it safely.

How you handle a crisis, such as problem behavior from an employee, is of considerable importance in maintaining positive work relationships. We have already suggested that the supervisor's response to an employee's problem behavior is an integral part of the process of behavior that either leads to changed positive behavior or to more unproductive behavior. If you explode when an employee misbehaves or if you go to pieces when there is a minor crisis developing, you may be creating conditions that will lead to even more problem behavior in the future. Taking a crisis like a test pilot or an astronaut may seem unnecessary, but the communication implications and aftermath effects of handling crises poorly can be costly.

Can You Make a Firm Decision After Reasonable Deliberation?   Do you jump at your first impulse in order to get the decision making over quickly? Do you search and search for more and more information, hoping the decision will be made for you?

Decisions made too quickly, or too slowly, may reflect an insecurity with the quality of the information you receive. Waiting too long to make a decision can bring on or aggravate a case of information overload. There's simply too much information being logjammed while you fail to clear the way.

In either case, practice the following seven simple steps to effective decision making.

1. Determine your objective and how it's to be measured.
2. Define the conditions and limits.
3. Gather information.
4. Identify feasible alternatives.
5. Weigh or evaluate alternatives.
6. Select the best alternatives.
7. Implement the chosen alternatives and follow through.

These steps aren't foolproof, but they are the professional way to make decisions.

Can You Leave Your Work at Work?   Managing is not an eight-to-five job. It requires enthusiasm, dedication, involvement, personal commitment, and much more. If you're effective at your job, you work long hours, take work home after hours, and spend at least part of your vacation on the phone checking on things in the shop. Although all this dedication is admirable, it also holds the potential for some serious problems.

See how much of this true story fits you. A vice-president of a large West Coast bank faced a dilemma. His annual vacation was approaching, and he was too busy to get away for even a week, yet like all bank employees, he was required to take a minimum one-week vacation every year. During that time, employees were not permitted inside the bank, even on personal business and in "civilian" clothes. The purpose of this policy was, of course, to prevent an employee engaged in some shady dealing from covering his tracks. To be effective, the policy included everyone in the bank, from janitor to president.

Our friendly vice-president wasn't pulling any creative banking escapades. He was avoiding a vacation simply because he was too busy, too involved in important ongoing projects. His solution?

For the full week of his enforced vacation, he set himself up in the back booth of a restaurant across the street from the bank. Every day between 10:00 A.M. and 2:00 P.M., dressed as always in a three-piece suit, he would visit with his colleagues over lunch. Every day between 10:00 A.M. and 2:00 P.M. his employees would one by one troop across the street, files and printouts in hand, to confer with their exiled leader. He was running his divisions as though he'd never left. Hopefully, such behavior is not typical of most organizations—but is it?

Aside from the ethical issues involved in short-circuiting a company policy, this man was a classic example of a "workaholic." He is physically incapable of leaving his work at work, even for a short period. He will bend and break rules rather than admit that no one (including himself) is indispensable. Apparently he is convinced that without him on the job every day of the week, his bank will fold.

Time away from the job, mentally and physically, is important for giving a person a sense of perspective. Without some time away, there's a danger of being too close to the trees to see the shape of the forest. Perhaps with this thought and the publicity of previous administrators in mind, Jimmy Carter addressed this very issue early in his presidency. He suggested that, although he would demand much of his staff, he also knew the value of time away from work spent with family and friends. He demanded that his staff follow his example and from time to time leave work at work in favor of other pursuits. It's good advice for management people, just as it was good advice for cabinet officers and White House staff.

CONCLUSION

Every manager should know her own strengths and weaknesses—and should be taking positive steps to enhance the strengths and correct the weaknesses. Few of us are favored with strengths and abilities in interviewing, counseling, and firing. At best, we may shine in one area, do OK in another, and do poorly in the third.

In each of the following sections, look for tactics or strategies that enhance your present skills.

Many of the topics in the following chapters flow one from another. For example, the need for handling problem employees, managing conflicts, and offering counseling often stems from poor selection. The need to fire people—especially those who deserve to be fired—often stems from inadequate or inappropriate managerial responses to problem behavior. In short, managers who study and turn into practice the topics in one section of this book may be able to head off having to put into operation the tactics in the following section.

HIRING

2
Looking for the "Right" Employee

Managing people successfully often depends on getting the right people. This is not to suggest that a manager's job is solely based on the luck of the draw, or that a manager with poorly selected employees is automatically doomed to failure. Still, many of a manager's problems with employees do come from the fact that some employees should not be doing the jobs they currently do, or that certain people should not have been placed in the part of the organization in which they now work. All management experts agree that a major expense for every organization is the unnecessary hiring, training, disciplining, and shuffling of employees, sadly followed by their termination. There is no denying that the "ins" of management must also have their "outs." It is possible, however, to minimize some of the unnecessary work, stress, and expense involved in such a revolving door by carefully matching the organization, the jobs it has to offer, the managers, and the employees.

There will never be a system that is 100 percent foolproof. Some employees will seem to possess the perfect mix of skill, talent, ability, and compatability. They will, after careful and thorough interviewing, appear to be precisely what the organization and its management are looking for. Further, these "perfect" employees will also feel that the organization they are joining, and the assignments they are being given, are just right for their career and personal aspirations. And yet, something apparently goes wrong, and things fail to work out as planned. Just as one cannot learn everything there is to know about a potential spouse from a few dates, a manager cannot expect to eliminate all potential employee problems when hiring. But reducing some of the potential problems is possible and very profitable. It can be done in part by carefully defining the nature of the jobs people are being given and in part by careful construction of the job specifications that lay out the qualifications required for the person doing a job. This is an important function of a personnel department, and one that all managers should have a feel for.

BEHAVIORAL MODELS

Reducing some of the problems with employees on the job can also be accomplished by matching the personalities and emotional profiles of employees with the realities and demands of the organization and the departments in which the new employees will work. This requires some sort of behavioral model, and there are several available. These models have the following common characteristics:

1. They are realistic. It does little good for a model of employee behavior to provide the manager with an insight into an employee's personality type if that personality type is rarely found, or if that personality type is hard to recognize. Realism demands that the personality types described relate to real people.

2. They are based on thorough research, carefully analyzed and reported. Sloppy research procedures can lead a manager to assume that certain kinds of employees will always behave in predictable ways, when in fact only those employees identical to the ones in the researcher's test will behave in a predictable way.

3. They provide answers, instead of just insights. Managers are held accountable for the bottom line, the final outcome of their actions. Any model of behavior, to be of any use, must give common-sense answers to a manager's basic questions about potential job performance or potential reaction to certain strategies for motivation and behavior control.

Let us look at two such models of personality types—one from Robert Presthus, the other from Charles Hughes and Vincent Flowers. Each model is from a different management expert, and each model describes certain kinds of behavior that one might expect from those employees who fit the profiles. Neither model is 100 percent accurate in predicting how a person with certain characteristics will behave on the job, or how she will respond to certain managerial strategies. Each of these models of employee personality will help managers involved in hiring and later problem solving determine some of the potential behaviors of the persons with whom they deal.

Robert Presthus's research led to the definition of three different types of personality, which he labled the "upward mobile," the "indifferent," and the "ambivalent."[1] Let's look at some of the characteristics of each.

The Upward Mobile

The upward mobile employee is the person who wants to move up in the organization and is motivated by a desire to achieve. This person wants the rewards such achievement can bring, and he is willing to pay whatever price is required for such achievement. The price of upward mobility in any organization will vary, but it usually involves working long hours at lower pay with a consequent loss of family time or time to pursue personal interests and hobbies. The price many organizations require usually includes loyalty and commitment to the organization and its goals, objectives, and policies. The upward mobile person is willing—even eager—to respond in a positive way to the demands of the organization.

This sort of person should be very easy to supervise, and most are. They will usually do anything their manager asks, and they will often find ways to improve on the methods and procedures currently being used. The manager blessed with this type of employee must remember that the upward mobile is motivated by achievement. He is therefore constantly looking for indications that others are aware of his skill, ability, performance, and dedication. Managers should give positive feedback often and should also give negative feedback when necessary, since the upward-mobile person wants to make whatever corrections are necessary to improve his chances for achievement. As we develop further in our chapter on communication in performance appraisal, we will see that such criticism should be sandwiched between positive feedback and should also be accompanied by suggestions of specific things the employee can do to improve. In short, communications with the upward mobile should be open, honest, and direct, more so than with either of the other two employee types.

Although the upward-mobile employee must seem like the ideal problem-free employee managers dream about, problems may arise. The upward mobile is often ridiculed by other employees as a "company man," or the "house errand boy." In some situations the upward mobile is clearly the person on the way up and is resented by other employees who may fall into one of the other groups. Also, because of their dedication and skill, upward mobiles are often paid more than less-motivated employees. This can create friction within the work group and can pose serious motivation problems for their manager.

Upward mobility poses another familiar problem for managers in departments where employees are organized by a labor union. Since the upward mobile employee is motivated to move up in the hierarchy, a good question is "which hierarchy?" If it's the company, few real motivation or communication problems result. If it's the union, the upward mobility of an employee can lead to a variety of conflicts. As in management, an employee who wants to move up in the union organization must be committed to the goals and policies of that organization. He must develop visibility within the union. Visibility usually requires that the employee stand out in labor-management disputes, taking the strong union position against management. An ambitious shop steward or local representative can serve his own interests by maintaining an obvious state of agitation and will eagerly capitalize on supervisory errors, slips, and miscommunications. Thus, employee upward mobility isn't always a bed of roses for a supervisor.

Another problem for supervisors is the upward mobile who has reached what Lawrence Peter calls the "level of incompetence." His "Peter Principle"[2] suggests that individuals who are upward mobile will continue to move up in an organization until they finally get themselves into a job or position where they're incapable of further upward movement. This last position becomes the individual's "level of incompetence." When an upward mobile "taps out," she is likely to pose something of a motivation problem for management, since the individual still wants to achieve but cannot go any further. This often causes the individual to change from an upward mobile to an ambivalent, presenting new subsequent difficulties for her manager. Faced with such an employee, managers can motivate by putting the individual into situations where her *past* accomplishments and contributions can be recognized. A manager of airline personnel faced just such a problem with a cabin attendant whose upward mobility had been halted. The employee had advanced as far in the airline organization as it was possible for her to advance. Her performance on her present job was adequate, but it was obvious to both her and her superiors that any further mobility was out of the question. As this fact began to sink in, the formerly upward mobile employee began to change into a problem employee. She was too valuable for the airline to lose, but motivating her with the prospect of future advancement was impossible. Her boss took our advice and began to involve the employee in developing training programs for new flight crews. By recognizing the employee's past accomplishments and wide experience, the manager was able to redirect the employee's efforts in a productive but clearly nonmobile direction. Upward mobiles, once they cease to be upwardly mobile, need to have their egos soothed. They need confirmation that their past efforts were valued and that their experience and present contributions are important to the organization. With this form of upward-mobile employee, a manager's communications should be in the form of counseling, with emphasis on the manager's use of listening skills. At this stage of her career, the upward mobile needs to feel a part of the larger organization. Wise managers provide this contact with an open, willing-to-listen attitude.

One final problem upward mobiles sometimes cause their managers is competition. Because an upward mobile wants to move up, the logical next step is to take the manager's job. Hopefully, this won't happen until the supervisor is moved up to a more responsible position and a vacancy is left for the upward-mobile employee to fill. However, some managers feel threatened by competent upwardly mobile employees. They do everything possible to confuse, confound, and otherwise restrict their best people from getting visibility in the organization. Managers who feel the pressure of competition from their employees will often do everything in their power to avoid hiring people who present any sort of challenge to their managerial position. This can, of course, work against you, since many top management people look at such actions as signals that a manager is on shaky ground. The top executive in a large manufacturing company in Indiana once observed in a management seminar that the only supervisors he would promote were those with enough confidence in their ability to hire people better than themselves. It takes a lot of self-confidence to hire upward-mobile employees. Yet, despite the potential threat, there is also a benefit for the manager who does. As the upward mobile performs her job well, such performance helps the department meet and exceed its performance standards. This will make her boss look good and improve her chances for promotion and recognition.

Although the upward-mobile employee seldom causes any severe management problems, unfortunately the same thing can't be said about the other two types of employees, the indifferent and the ambivalent.

The Indifferent

The indifferent personality is quite different from the upward mobile. He presents some interesting and perplexing problems for supervisors. The indifferent is a person motivated by a desire to have satisfactory interpersonal relationships, although this individual usually prefers to maintain and enjoy such relationships off the job rather than on the job. The indifferent personality type rejects both the rewards and the pressures of the organization. In fact, many indifferents really have no strong feelings about their organization for or against. They aren't committed to the organization's goals, and they reject the usual ego rewards the organization can provide (such as advancement or recognition or power). Nor do they dislike their organization. What they want is a clear and understandable set of job performance standards, an acceptable wage, and the mental freedom to pursue nonwork interests. The indifferent person will be likely to reject any attempt by management to involve him in the decision-making processes. Instead, the indifferent usually prefers to be told what to do and then to be left alone to do it. The indifferent is not always a problem employee, only one who won't respond positively to the usual organizational reward system. Some indifferents are found in high skill positions, and they may take great pride in their achievements. However, they are not interested in any organizational reward except the salary, benefits, and quality supervision the organization usually provides.

Indifferent employees are far less willing to communicate with their superiors than are the upward mobiles, except when relating as a person to another person. Indifferents are unlikely to offer suggestions or to share perceptions or personal feelings with management. They do value their interpersonal relations with others. They are best motivated by having their boss maintain as much as possible a tension-free environment in which the job can be done as painlessly as possible.

Since the indifferent rejects competition for advancement, he is far more likely to take a somewhat callous or suspicious view of his manager, especially if the manager is perceived as an upward-mobile person. Thus, the stage can be set for some severe personality clashes. To combat or avoid such clashes, you should be aware of the need most indifferents have for structure and order in their work assignments. Also, keep in mind that, although the indifferent person may reject symbols of status, he nevertheless wants to be treated as an individual and not as a member of a faceless herd. This can lead to many communication problems, brought on by the indifferent who seems to want plaudits for simply doing his regular, routine job, even if that job is done in an average, run-of-the-mill way. This often antagonizes managers, who may feel that it's not appropriate to commend or praise a person for simply doing the expected or the mediocre. Because of an indifferent attitude toward work and the workplace, manager and employee might clash over various job standards, including absenteeism, lateness, and personal behavior on the job. Because indifferents really don't care whether or not they come to work, their absenteeism and tardiness levels are far greater than those of either of the other groups. And just as they are likely to not show up for work, they'll often give an indifferent excuse for their failure to come in. For an upward-mobile manager the indifferent can be both a challenge and a mystery.

The Ambivalent

Managing the ambivalent personality often requires a manager with the listening and counseling abilities of a professional psychiatrist. The ambivalent is the person torn between a desire for personal freedom and a desire for the rewards of upward mobility, without "paying the price" for either. Left alone, an ambivalent person can become mentally ill, in effect, pulled in two directions at once. Yet, although the true ambivalent remains a constant source of problems for most managers, some degree of ambivalence can be found in the personality of all individuals, yours and your employees. Few of us, no matter how upwardly mobile, are willing to pay an unlimited price for organizational rewards. Each of us at some point ceases to be upwardly mobile.

However, just because a person reaches his limit does not mean that he will not be motivated by additional rewards from the company or the boss. This condition is similar to that of the upward-mobile person who reaches his level of incompetence while still wishing to maintain upward mobility.

The ambivalent person presents some new problems for managers by resenting upward mobiles for their success while maintaining an aloofness toward the indifferents. The ambivalent person often "enjoys" poor interpersonal relationships in much the same way the hypochondriac "enjoys" poor health. The ambivalent also tends to believe that those who achieve some measure of success on the job (upward mobiles) or off the job (indifferents) do so because of blind luck. The ambivalent is often unwilling to admit that talent, hard work, or dedication have any part in such success, especially the success earned by the upward mobile. Ambivalents are often more intelligent than either their upward-mobile or indifferent co-workers, and they like to frequently display their intelligence, especially at the expense of their co-workers. The ambivalent employee is one who must be managed with a firm hand, but with some sensitivity as well. The problem facing managers is often a reluctance to face up to the demands of the ambivalent for special considerations due him because of real or imagined feelings of being "underpaid, underloved, and underfed." The ambivalent can and often does resort to immature behavior and requires that managers maintain close communication contact and control over him.

The above three types of employee and supervisory personalities give us some interesting clues about human behavior on the job and what communication strategies might be most appropriate for managing each type. There is another set of employee and manager types, developed by Charles Hughes and Vincent Flowers,[3] which can give us some interesting and useful insights into the behavior of our employees. We'll also find some additional ways we might do a better job of motivating our employees by matching our management style to each employee's personality.

The Boss
as a Communication Model

When looking at the link between manager and employee, we find an interesting reaction of employees to various forms of job enrichment. Regardless of the job enrichment strategy used by an organization, employees usually judge the quality of their job by the quality of their boss. When the boss helps create a positive climate in a department, demonstrates competence, or manages in a way the employee can appreciate, employees express satisfaction with their jobs. When the boss is "inappropriate," employees appear unmotivated and complain about the need for some sort of job enrichment. This notion lends further emphasis to the importance of analyzing your employees' personalities and adjusting your management and communication strategy to fit.

EMPLOYEE PERSONALITY TYPES

Many of the costly programs designed to improve morale and communication in organizations seem to fail for no obvious or apparent reasons.

A possible approach to solving this problem is to analyze employee personality and behavior in terms of six broad types of individuals. With these types, it is then possible to develop and use communication strategies directly suited to the individual's needs and motivations. Not everyone agrees with this approach. Some experts have difficulty pigeonholing people according to some arbitrary set of personality types. One psychologist even goes so far as to suggest that, where you set up jobs with different complexities, you must set up different work systems for all. It simply doesn't work if you push people into slots without any options. Throughout this book, we have consistently rejected the notion that all people are alike; nevertheless, it does managers little good to study communication and human behavior if there are no generalities that can be drawn. Therefore, when we look at various personality types and the appropriate communication response to them, we assume such generalizations are merely guides for appropriate managerial behavior.

An assumption made by most managers is that there is bound to be some measure of clashing or hostility between individuals in any work situation, no matter how harmonious the manager tries to make it. Because of this fact of organizational life, you may find it useful to make yourself aware of how to communicate with various types of employees. The importance of this communication relationship between employee and manager is underscored by our earlier observation that most employees judge the quality and desirability of their jobs in terms of whether they feel they have a good boss or a bad boss. Thus, even when you try to provide employees with growth opportunities, many of these employees may simply choose to ignore them, remaining indifferent to such involvement attempts.

We have already examined how certain groups or types of employees are motivated by different things. Let's next consider a more detailed set of employee types. Recognize that, just as with the personality types we've already discussed, no one individual fits neatly or completely into any category, even though most of us have one set of type characteristics that predominate. The six types are as follows:

Tribalistic

Although accounting for one-fourth of the population, the group of tribalistic types includes some 40 percent of all hourly production workers. Most comfortable with an established ritual, members of this group take pride in working for a prominent company. For them, it is like being a member of a strong tribe.

They generally have little or no ambition to rise out of their group, and they interpret most of their job in the context of whether they have a good or a bad boss. They will attach themselves to a good boss and often will go to him for assistance—even after he has been placed in a different job.

The most effective way to motivate tribalistic workers is to provide them with a boss they will respect. If you are their boss and can't relate to them, find their natural leader and get him on your side. You can't ask them to make decisions, but if you work out a procedure together, they will follow it.

They will also interpret working conditions as a sign that management cares about them, so they will respond to a modern office or shop. Because their "future" extends only a few weeks out, meaningful compensation means money, not retirement or deferred payments.

Egocentric

Although dominant in only about 10 percent of the manufacturing population, the egocentric group's traits are found in some degrees in almost all people—and a few drinks will usually reveal these traits. Culturally disadvantaged persons are often egocentric, and the incidence among these people in prison is extremely high.

Often carrying an impressive-looking bankroll (a hundred-dollar bill on the outside of the roll), a person in this group is usually physically strong but not necessarily aggressive, is likely to become a union organizer, has no conception of company loyalty, and is apt to walk out on the job or fail to show up.

He is usually a malcontent and extremely suspicious. He interprets good working conditions as a trick by management to get him to work harder. To this person, his pay is never enough, only what the company has been forced to pay him; however, straight pay is the only compensation he understands. He needs hard rules and will respond to firmness and threats of demotion or loss of pay. He will take full advantage of an easygoing boss.

Conformist

Surveys indicate that conformists have become less common during the last ten years, but 40 percent of hourly workers still get this label.

Conformists believe that all employees should do their jobs as the company asks. They appreciate good working conditions, but will not complain about bad ones. They usually will rebel when they are asked to bend or break a rule.

Effective management of conformists is keyed to a clear set of rules. By nature, they will obey rules without question and will point them out to others. They are comfortable with time clocks because the timecards are reminders that they get to work on time.

Manipulative

The manipulative types are the achievers, the wheeler-dealers who play all the angles and reap the rewards. Sometimes aggressive and overbearing, the manipulative person earns big money in sales and leadership positions, but his ethics are flexible; for example, he is likely to take orders he knows the factory can't fill.

Motivating him is no problem: Show him where the cheese is, and he'll find his way through the maze. The need for performance review and other analysis decreases as his achievement realization increases, but money and the status symbols that go with success are important to him.

A manipulator's motivation can be destroyed, however, by putting in career-path courses or other internal guidance and counseling situations that aim for conformity. This tends to negate his potential.

One problem: The manipulator can be abrasive, especially when managing almost all other psychological types. One strategy to overcome this is to point out his "personal barriers to success in this company" and to offer to pay his expenses for management development courses or any other approach he thinks will help him to solve his problem.

"Don't expect to change things" is one of the worst things you can tell a manipulator because changing things probably is one of his prime goals.

Reprimands usually don't bother him because he will react by showing that he is producing and merely has to cut a few corners to get results.

Sociocentric

The sociocentric type is primarily concerned with the welfare of mankind, preventing stress and strife, and generally keeping the peace. This group is growing, especially among the young. Ralph Nader is their ideal and model.

Low wages don't bother them if they believe that their company is helping humanity and the work is socially acceptable, but they will form a union and oppose the company if they think it is persecuting workers or others.

They can be motivated by being shown how their work benefits fellow employees and other groups. They respond best to a boss who is agreeable and gets people working together in a spirit of friendship without many orders being issued.

Sociocentric workers are the ones most likely to be motivated by group job enrichment programs, as long as they don't have to make too many individual decisions. They have little desire to move into management because they are too tolerant of others and dislike pigeon-holding people in categories.

Most effective among the various forms of compensation for sociocentrics are hospital and medical insurance, pension plans, and other elements of paternalism—which these workers like for their social, not their economic, value.

Existential

Traditionally found in areas such as research, members of the existential group are now part of the new breed of managers. Great creativity is the existential employee's major contribution to the company.

Strictly a lone wolf, sufficient unto herself, the existential worker is indifferent to physical working conditions, but chafes under restrictions and rebels against regimentation. Although she performs better when left on a loose leash, she has a tendency to wander off on tangents unrelated to company objectives and must be checked periodically.

She is motivated by doing work of her own choosing that is

challenging and requires imagination. Programs on career development, management by objectives, and communications must be extremely flexible. The teamwork aspects of job enrichment hold no appeal, but the greater responsibility does.

Money is important, but primarily because of the freedom it permits. The existential employee dislikes being financially dependent on a company. Flextime, portable pensions, and other plans that contribute a measure of freedom are appealing to her.

In Table 1 we have summarized each of these six types, along with some comments about how each type might be motivated and how managers should respond in developing a positive work climate. To find out which type you are, answer the questions in Figure 1. This is a demonstration test only and is intended to give you a "feel" for the way the system operates. It is based on attitudes in personal life and not in work—which in 80 percent of all cases are different. To score the test, count the number of statements circled next to each letter and enter in Figure 2 the total for each. The totals for the number of circles and checks will give you a general indication of your personality pattern.

Now that we've examined each of these six types, a logical question might be: What should managers do to effectively manage employees in each of these groups?

FIGURE 1. A self-test of employee types: Which type are you?

There are six choices for each question. There are no right or wrong answers; simply circle the statement you like best. If you have a second choice, place a check by it also.

1. A family should
   a. Stay close together and take care of one another.
   b. Let each person go his own way without interference.
   c. Provide guidance to the younger members on what is right and wrong.
   d. Help each other succeed in a career and see that the children get ahead in the world.
   e. Provide warmth and harmony among all the members and their friends.
   f. Permit family life to be like real life, with all of its good and bad points.

2. Freedom is
   a. Not having to worry about money and other problems.
   b. Not being pushed around by people who have more power or money.
   c. The chance to work and live where I want and be a good citizen of the community.
   d. The opportunity to do and to pursue success.
   e. The right of people to be themselves without prejudice and social differences.
   f. Doing what I like to do without denying others their freedom.

3. A good job is
   a. Having a good boss regardless of the work.
   b. One that pays enough money.
   c. Knowing exactly what should be done.
   d. Where good work leads to promotion.
   e. Working with a good group of people.
   f. Solving interesting problems.

FIGURE 1. A self-test of employee types. (Continued)

4. Laws are
   a. To tell us what to do and protect us from people.
   b. Not important unless you get caught breaking them.
   c. Necessary to keep order in society and should be obeyed by everyone.
   d. Sometimes unnecessarily restrictive in getting things done.
   e. Useful if they promote social causes.
   f. Necessary to make any society function.

5. Money means
   a. Paying for the things I need to keep going.
   b. Buying things that make me feel important.
   c. Security for the present and future and a good standard of living.
   d. Power and status and belongings that I have earned.
   e. Social distance and barriers in society.
   f. Freedom and opportunity to be myself.

6. Personal possessions
   a. Are necessary for living.
   b. Make me feel like someone important.
   c. Come from hard work and should go only to people who deserve them.
   d. Are a sign of success and a source of pride.
   e. Are not as important as personal friendships.
   f. Are important only for what they mean to the individual.

7. A good boss
   a. Tells me what he wants done and helps me do it.
   b. Is tough, but lets me be tough also.
   c. Sets clear policies and sees that people follow them.
   d. Helps me understand the objectives and rewards me when I achieve them.
   e. Is more of a friend than a boss.
   f. Sets goals with me, then trusts me to do the job the best way.

FIGURE 2. Scoresheet for Figure 1.

Response	Represents		Totals
a	Tribalistic	_____	_____
b	Egocentric	_____	_____
c	Conformist	_____	_____
d	Manipulative	_____	_____
e	Sociocentric	_____	_____
f	Existential	_____	_____

Some Supervisor Do's and Don'ts

It's not possible for a manager to respond to all employees in a way that will automatically insure accurate and motivating communication.

Still, there are some general comments about your communications that can help you relate to your employees.

THE TRIBALISTIC EMPLOYEE

The tribalistic employee works best in an environment where there are precise rules that everyone understands. The tribalistic person wants a manager who will behave in the manner of a benevolent autocrat. You should maintain a firm, friendly attitude toward the tribalistic employee. Communication should be simple, clear, and direct, with as little intellectualizing as possible. This individual is a prime target for the reassurance messages we discussed in earlier chapters. The reassurance you offer should stress the stability of the environment and the employee's place in that stable environment. The tribalistic employee appreciates a manager who will make decisions and who will relate to him in clear, nontechnical language.

THE EGOCENTRIC EMPLOYEE

In many ways, the egocentric employee is similar to the tribalistic, although he may not need as much protective reassurance from you. An egocentric employee is tough and aggressive. Assume (or at least give the impression you assume) that this employee doesn't want to work. Your communications should be brief and to the point, with no hint of softness or hesitation. A new supervisor in an air-conditioning plant assessed his employees as predominantly egocentric. To deal with them, he always talked quickly and directly and moved briskly throughout his department looking straight ahead. This show of bravado, he felt, would help his tough "give'm hell" message. It worked well, too, until one day he breezed across the department looking dead ahead, strode up to a door, briskly threw it open, and went inside—straight into the broom closet. His red face when he came out—and the grins and cheers from his employees in the shop—suggested that a little less aggressiveness might be in order.

THE CONFORMIST EMPLOYEE

The conformist seems to work best in an atmosphere with structure and some semblance of goal-directed management. Managers of conformist employees should be well organized. Give the impression that you know where they're going and what you expect from them. Since the conformist is loyal, she expects loyalty in return from both the organization and the supervisor. With this type of employee, be careful to avoid comments and statements that suggest disrespect for tradition or for company policies. Slick or avant garde management techniques should be avoided in favor of traditional methods.

TABLE 1. Six Employee Types and What Makes Them Tick

	TRIBALISTIC	EGOCENTRIC	CONFORMIST	MANIPULATIVE	SOCIOCENTRIC	EXISTENTIAL
Percentage of managers, based on studies of 1,707 supervisors	10	10	20	20	15	25
Percentage of hourly personnel	40	10	40	5	5	almost none
Percentage of general population	25	10	35	10	10	10
Key identifying attitude on reasons for importance of money today	Buys groceries, pays for rent and other things I need to keep going.	Buys things I want and makes me feel like somebody.	Allows me to save for rainy day, have decent standard of living, and aid the unfortunate.	Is a measure of success in my job, my company, and my community.	Enables me to enjoy many friendships and support worthwhile causes.	By itself, not as important as how it is used. It gives me freedom and chance to be myself.
Most effective management climate	Good boss, no decision making, rules to follow, plenty of security, pensions. Regular pay, no piecework. Work groups of ten maximum. Short-cycle work.	Freedom of action to a point but clear line of authority. Piecework pay. No intangibles or deferred compensation.	Rewards for seniority and loyal service. Rules and procedures for everything. Organization charts and career planning.	Keep light rein. Allow innovation. Give status symbols, decision-making authority.	Group meetings and participation. No stress or conflict. Highlights socially useful purpose of operation. Friendly supervisors.	Loose structure. Stimulate creativity. Spell out long-range goals. De-emphasize retirement plans and other "golden-handcuffs."

	TRIBALISTIC	EGOCENTRIC	CONFORMIST	MANIPULATIVE	SOCIOCENTRIC	EXISTENTIAL
Most effective motivators	Good boss, steady pay. Job content irrelevant.	Hard cash; leave him alone.	Regular advancement by seniority. Clear procedures. Efficient management system, appraisal reviews.	Opportunity to wheel and deal. Options in pension and retirement. Money. Status symbols.	Harmonious working environment. De-emphasize merit pay and "climbing the corporate ladder."	Continuously challenging work. Freedom of choice. Job-enrichment programs.
Comment	Little desire for advancement. Will resist transfer. Recession brings converts.	High turnover. Always discontented. Recession brings converts from other groups. Highly suspicious.	Size dwindling rapidly due to broadening horizons of mass media, but reinforced by tradition. Found in bureaucracies.	Sex, poker, religion are all games. Flexible ethics. Best as salesmen.	If they see the company is hurting people, they will organize and rebel.	Increasingly found in management. Incompatible with tribalistic, egocentric, or conformist boss.

THE MANIPULATIVE EMPLOYEE

The manipulative employee demands treatment as an individual. She wants to be included in any process involving her personal goals. With this person, you must appear to have carefully thought-out strategies for managing. As a "game player," the manipulative employee expects you to constantly be one-up. The best approach is to stress status and to tie motivational and instructional messages to the individual's career goals and aspirations. On the other hand, the manipulative individual is likely to reject orders or instructions that are based solely on company policies and procedures. The manipulative employee wants to be persuaded or convinced. Given rational and personally meaningful answers and information, the manipulative employee is apt to respond in a positive way.

THE SOCIOCENTRIC EMPLOYEE

The sociocentric values group identification. He wants and needs to be considered as part of a group—although not necessarily the same groups the supervisor might identify with. The sociocentric will probably respond best to opportunities for group participation in problem solving and in job enrichment strategies that stress group rather than individual activity. You should communicate in a friendly, open way designed to create a personal bond of employee acceptance. However, if the sociocentric feels you are using friendly communications as part of a "power politics" strategy, such messages may be rejected.

THE EXISTENTIAL EMPLOYEE

The existential is perhaps the ultimate individual. He responds best to individual forms of job enrichment and demands that management accept his individuality. Appeals to the common good or what's best for the entire department won't work with the existential. Neither will instruction from the supervisor stating "this is what you should do." As a free and independent thinker, the existential wants you to provide access to information while letting him make the actual decision. To the extent that it is possible, leave the existential alone—assuming there is enough information available for him to make good decisions.

Clearly, we've opened some possible areas for conflict, since most managers fall into the existential, manipulative, or conformist categories. When a manager of one type is communicating with an employee of another type, there are bound to be distortions and misunderstandings. By testing your own motivations (with the table and the questionnaire in this chapter) you should have a better grasp of your frame of reference. With a little of the same kind of analysis applied to your present and prospective employees, it's possible to avoid or more easily overcome many of the factors that cause some employees to fall into the "problem" category.

A note of caution. Formal testing of personality, either of prospective employees or present employees, may be considered an unfair labor practice. Further, there are some serious questions of ethics involved when managers undertake to probe into the psyche of employees. We are not suggesting that managers actually submit present or prospective employees to personality tests of the sort discussed in this chapter. At best, such testing would be an unwarranted invasion of an individual's privacy. We are suggesting that there is a direct relationship between the compatability of an employee and his or her manager and the employee's satisfaction with and performance on the job. Hiring an individual who seems to have a personality that conflicts with the prevailing personality mix in a department or organization is an invitation to future problems. This seems to place each manager in a dilemma: to evaluate personality or not to evaluate personality?

There is no firm rule, and many organizations do use expensive and sophisticated psychological tests when screening new employees. A discussion of this is beyond the range of this book. We do suggest that managers take the following approach with regard to the personality types discussed in this chapter.

1. Examine your own personality—realistically.
2. Using the information in this chapter and your knowledge of the people now working for you, see if you can put names and faces on the personality types we have been discussing. This will help you to adapt the models to your people.
3. When interviewing an individual for a position—either someone new to the organization or someone being considered for a transfer or promotion—try putting her into the categories in the above model. See if the new employees match the personalities of those with whom they will be working—including their new manager.

Such an assessment process is not foolproof, nor is it very scientific, but according to those who have tried it, it does work. It is an extension and refinement of the sizing up that takes place whenever anyone is being considered for a job. Properly used, a model of various personality types can be a useful addition to the interviewing process.

3
Reviewing Resumes And Application Forms

Most persons applying for managerial, technical, or professional positions today have prepared a personal resume. Schools and special seminars on resume preparation give detailed instruction on the best ways to go about such a task. In addition, most firms ask job applicants to complete an application form. Usually a resume or application form is a prospective employer's first exposure to a job candidate. The questions on a job application will probably result in fairly predictable kinds of information, and thus they require somewhat less analysis. Resumes, on the other hand, are written with no firm rules or guidelines, and they are designed to advertise the applicant's skills, abilities, and potential. They are *not supposed* to be comprehensive work/career "histories." And although even the best-designed application form will turn up some "creative truth," it is on the self-prepared resume that such creativity is taken to new heights. In this chapter, we will examine those parts of job application forms and applicant resumes that should be most closely reviewed, and we will raise issues and questions that should be kept in mind as resumes and application forms are reviewed.

WHAT IS A RESUME?

A resume is an unstructured biographical summary of an individual's work, school, and personal career. It can be written in hundreds of styles and formats with virtually limitless variations. There are several kinds of resumes.

The General Resume

The general resume gives a fairly comprehensive review of major parts of an individual's life. Sections usually include personal data; education; work or career experience; military service; special skills, licenses, and training; hobbies and interests; location preferences; and a job or career objective. This is the most common resume form used for job seeking. Dated items (education, work experience, military service) are usually written in reverse chronological order—the most recent experiences listed first.

The Functional Resume

The functional resume is favored by persons undertaking a second career, those trying to move from one career area to another, and those with large gaps in their work histories. (Most notable in this last category are women returning to the work force after several years of being employed only in their homes.) In a functional resume, chronological order is abandoned in favor of a listing of activities the applicant has undertaken—on and off the job. Activities are usually listed with action words, such as *planned, supervised, co-ordinated, responsible for.*

Persons with military experience are often advised to use a functional resume to translate military job jargon into understandable civilian terms.

The Introduction Resume

The introduction is a short biography, usually written in prose format. It details an individual's major experiences and accomplishments. It is prepared as a biography, to be used for (1) speech introductions, (2) who's who directories and listings, (3) corporate directories, and (4) public relations and publicity.

Such resumes are rarely used for employment purposes, except perhaps for occasional employees such as consultants.

What to Look for

When reviewing resumes and job application forms, a screener or employer should be looking for two broad kinds of information:

1. Those facts that directly apply to the job for which the person is being considered and which bear favorably on her chances for employment.
2. Those facts that will automatically exclude an applicant from further consideration for a job.

The facts in the first category will vary from position to position and company to company. Each firm looks for different things from its applicants. Therefore, let us concentrate on some general danger signals one might find in typical resume and application form information. These signals do not automatically become "knockout" factors, but they do bear close scrutiny.

Use of a Functional Resume.   The functional resume may indicate periods of nonpaid employment or unemployment. Some of the reasons for such gaps may be indications of

1. Arrest and imprisonment.
2. Being fired.

3. General unwillingness to seek work.
4. Mental or physical illness.
5. Military service that ended with a less than honorable discharge.

Of course, such gaps may also be due to

1. Child bearing.
2. Employment in the home.
3. Volunteer church or community service.
4. Extensive travel.
5. Schooling—not otherwise accounted for in an "education" section.

Keep in mind that none of these ten reasons should automatically prevent a person from being considered for a position. However, they may prompt more insightful questions of the applicant (within the limitations set down in the law), to fill in the gaps and permit a more informed selection decision.

Specific Gaps Unaccounted for by Education or Employment.   One step-off to gaps is use of year dates, or no dates instead of month/year dates. We listed above some of the reasons for these gaps, which bear investigation or analysis.

Membership in Sexist, Racist, or Subversive Organization.   Membership in such organizations may suggest a biased point of view that is inconsistent with most managerial positions.

Labor Union Membership.   Labor union membership is a very sensitive topic. For some nonunion companies, the appearance of prior union membership indicates that the applicant is more inclined to favorably respond to a union organizing attempt. There is no hard data to support this view. Indeed, it is possible that the National Labor Relations Board (NLRB) would view a firm's attempt to avoid hiring persons who belong to labor unions as an unfair labor practice.

Membership in Organizations that Indicate Racial, Ethnic, Sex, or Age Characteristics, or Religious or Sexual Preferences.   Membership in organizations that indicate particular characteristics is another sensitive issue in hiring. Major civil rights and worker rights laws prohibit *all* discrimination in the areas of race, ethnicity, religious preferences, sex, age (over forty), and national origin. Many court decisions and state statutes have extended these protections to cover homosexuals. Asking in an application form for information bearing on any of these areas is specifically prohibited unless there is a bona fide job-related reason for doing so. In mentioning the issue here, we in no way encourage or condone any such prohibited discrimination; however, discrimination that works in favor of certain applicants may be a reason for a person to include such memberships in activities as:

> Black Student Union
> Knights of Columbus
> DeMolay
> B'nai Brith
> Hadassah
> Polish-American Club (or any ethnic-American club)
> United Baptist Ministries Association
> Tribal Council Director (Native Americans)

Resume writers will frequently use such memberships and associations as a way of informing prospective employers about their personal backgrounds. It is perfectly legal for an applicant to volunteer *any information* on a resume. It is legal to use such information when making a selection decision only when there is a bona fide job-related reason for doing so, or when such "positive discrimination" is used as part of an acceptable Affirmative Action program in an organization. If neither reason exists for using sensitive information in favor of an applicant, it may be wise to simply strike out any such information from resumes rather than have it appear in your applicant files.

Photograph Attached to a Resume.   Having an applicant's photo attached to a resume in an employer's selection files *may* constitute evidence of intent to discriminate—even if the employer did not solicit the photograph. Most cautious and fair-minded employers simply remove and destroy photographs before considering an applicant's resume.

Age.   The only basis for legal discrimination based on age is against those who are not yet legally adults in the state where they are being hired. Any other mention of age should be ignored in favor of those factors that indicate a person's ability to do a job well.

A Pattern of Job Hopping.   A pattern of job hopping appears as a succession of jobs, each held for relatively short periods. Job hopping patterns may indicate the following:

1.   A potentially troublesome employee.
2.   Inability to cooperate and work well with others.

3. Serious personal problems such as alcoholism or drug abuse.
4. Lack of maturity.
5. High technical ability in a short-supply job market. This individual job hops to improve salary and/or position. It may be a desirable characteristic, since such mobility usually comes only to those who are very competent and in demand. Such a pattern may also suggest lack of commitment to an organization in favor of personal goals.

Too Long, Excessive, or Inconsistent Record of Education. Some inconsistent patterns for education include the following:

1. A period of education much longer than that normally required for a particular career area.
2. A pattern of interrupted schooling.
3. Degrees or diplomas from areas other than those related in some way to the individual's apparent career plan.
4. A succession of schools attended with no apparent degrees or certificates awarded.
5. A significant gap between start and finish of a degree or certificate program.

Some of the reasons for an unusual education record include the following:

1. Military service, requiring frequent changes in residence.
2. A corporate transfer pattern that caused frequent relocations.
3. Military service or job demands that forced a long interruption in one's education.
4. Family responsibilities that either interrupted education or forced an individual to go to school part time.
5. A change in career goals or plans, resulting in unnecessary credits or degrees.
6. A desire for personal growth through formal education. For example, an individual with a master's degree in business administration who returns to school for a bachelor of arts degree in music or literature may be doing so as a means of personal growth and development.
7. Insufficient funds—making it necessary to stop school to earn tuition and living expenses.

All of these above are positive reasons for an unusual education pattern. Let's look at some negative reasons for such patterns:

1. Lack of maturity—an unwillingness to set and work toward goals.
2. Lack of motivation—no desire to do the work required to complete an academic program.

3. Shopping for a suitable program. This may be another indication of failure to set goals or to come to grips with career decision making.
4. Discipline or academic difficulties.

It should be noted that a pattern of changing academic activity should not be taken as a mark against an applicant. Today, most students and adults returning to school show some signs of changing programs, majors, and studies and have significant interruptions in their education. Such factors should merely raise questions in the reviewer's mind.

Work Experience That Does Not Correspond with Formal Education and Training.   An example of work experience differing from training is a person with a degree in forestry and considerable experience in public-service personnel work. Or an engineering degree combined with experience in counseling. Or a theology background and experience in real estate. There are three main reasons for noting such an apparent contradiction:

1. It may suggest an individual with wide-ranging, flexible tastes, preferences, and interests. Also, this person may possess hidden talents that may suit her to a particular position.
2. It may indicate a person unsure of goals and career desires, or even a person who has a diminished sense of self-confidence. We conducted interviews with several persons having this pattern of education and experience. The most common reason for not following the career path suggested by the person's formal training was a sense of incompetence or inability to handle the demands of that career area.
3. It may show the unfortunate result of poor counseling earlier in an individual's schooling. After four or more years of an unsuitable program, the hapless individual is trained for a career he does not want, and he is forced to find work elsewhere.

Of these reasons for contradictory education and work experience, (a) is a real plus, (b) a possible negative, and (c) a sad but neutral reality.

Education, Experience, or Personal Information Highlighted or Emphasized.   Most resume writing advice suggests that the writer emphasize certain parts of his background by

1. Putting them first in the resume.
2. Giving them more detail.
3. Using visual highlighters, such as capital letter typing, underlines, or extra spacing around the highlighted item.

There is no problem with highlighting, but there are some interesting considerations.

1. Noting what is highlighted can indicate what a person feels is his real strength.
2. An employer searching for a person with experience to share may want to take a cautious look at a person whose resume emphasizes education. Of course, the reverse is also true.
3. Highlighting has been used by some resume writers to divert attention from other areas the applicant considers her weak points. A reviewer may want to avoid being distracted in this way.

Military Service.   Work experience has long been valuable for developing mature individuals with job skills and leadership abilities. However, some employers may want to carefully review the nature of a person's military experiences in light of the requirements of a certain position. After major wars, all the uniformed services had difficulty with people whose talents were well suited to wartime, but ill suited to a peacetime bureaucracy.

A brilliant battlefield commander may not be right for a desk job requiring control over fairly routine activities. The best way most employers have found to deal with military service experience is to first identify the skills needed by the person who will do the job you are offering. Then review the applicant's military record, looking for evidence of those skills—or at least evidence that the applicant has experience in being assigned to areas where those skills were apt to have been used.

Some ex-military people translate their work experience into civilian terms, relying on descriptive words such as *supervised, controlled, coordinated,* etc. They also translate some of their military assignments, especially those that have no civilian counterpart, into terms that a nonmilitary person can understand. This adaptation is useful and indicates an applicant's willingness and desire to blend into a new career world. Other former military personnel have difficulty translating their experience into civilian terms. Two possible reasons for this inability are a lack of information about the nonmilitary world and military security restrictions.

The first reason may indicate an individual who will find a civilian career, especially one with managerial responsibilities, difficult to adapt to. She might do quite well in a field with clear-cut requirements, or in an organization where policies are reasonably precise. This does not mean that all former military people, or those former military who served through a career until retirement, are automatically unsuited to the freewheeling activities and responsibilities of the business sector. It does mean that a person who cannot (or perhaps will not) translate military language into civilian terms may have difficulties later on.

Some military people work in areas that are classified. They are not permitted to detail their working experiences, and in some cases they are not even permitted to disclose the exact part of the government where they worked. Employers should respect the national security requirements of those jobs and understand the burden these requirements can place on a well-qualified individual who wants to work in the civilian community. When security reasons are cited on a resume in place of actual job assignments or details, it is wise to consider the interview as the prime source of job-related information. In interviewing these persons, ask them to tell you what they feel they are permitted to disclose about their former military employment. Then ask questions that relate to the person's daily duties *as those duties relate to the job for which the person is applying.*

Hobbies and Interests.   Many people include on their resumes some mention of their hobbies and personal interests. Although such information is optional and usually not directly job related, it can provide some interesting and useful insights into the character, background, and potential of the applicant.

Some of the interesting things that one can observe in the person's listing of interests and hobbies are the following:

1. Job-related skills—or skills that can be used on the job. Examples might be ham radio enthusiasts or persons with hobbies requiring technical skills such as electronic assembly, computer programming, or model building.
2. Public speaking or exposition, writing, or editing can indicate a person with useful skills for the job.
3. Manual skills—assembling, artistic skills.
4. Athletic interests indicate a general state of good health. Note that some persons seem to feel that those who engage in solitary athletic activities (jogging, exercise, skiing) are less sociable that those who engage in team or group activities (tennis, baseball, golf). There is little evidence that such preferences actually do relate to a person's social skills, but combined with other information, such as interest listing could help fill out a pattern.
5. Social activities, such as card playing, group membership, or group activities may indicate organizational skills, along with some of the social skills mentioned above.
6. Persons who have excelled in hobbies, sports, or social pursuits may confront prospective employers with a potential problem. If these per-

sons are primarily committed to their hobby or interest, their work *may* suffer. As with so many of the things we should watch for on a person's resume, this should be taken only as an indication or possibility, not as an absolute prediction. If a resume shows considerable dedication to a hobby or interest, it might be useful to ask the applicant some searching "motive" questions during subsequent interviews.

Willingness to Relocate.   If an applicant indicates whether she is willing to relocate, fine. If there is no indication, look at the person's pattern of employment and schooling. A person who has been educated in a relatively small geographic area and has been working in the same area is unlikely to respond favorably to an offer to relocate.

References.   Resume writers are usually advised to indicate on their resumes that "references are available on request." Therefore, the absence of references should not be given much importance.

When reviewing references, keep in mind that the applicant is unlikely to list anyone who might give a negative or unfavorable reference. For this reason, many employees prefer to seek references from former employers, teachers, or supervisors.

If you do review references, look for the following:

1. The mix of social and business or professional references. This can be viewed as a subtle indication of what part of the applicant's life history he values most.

2. The use of family references. It may indicate a person who is having difficulty finding "suitable" nonfamily references and might suggest closer scrutiny of former employers, etc.

3. The use of references of persons in the same job field or profession as the job for which the person is applying. Such references may indicate some greater degree of motivation than one would find in a person who knows little or nothing about the job and its requirements.

4. The request that you not contact certain references. Many prospective employees understandably do not want their present employers to know they are looking for another job. However, reluctance to have other references contacted may be a signal of trouble and bears further investigation.

5. Religious, philosophical, or political references. May be used as a form of name-dropping. The danger here is that if you find yourself favorably or unfavorably swayed by such references, you may find yourself later subjected to charges of favoritism or discrimination. When such references do appear on or accompany a résumé, be careful how you use them.

Availability.   Unless otherwise noted, it is reasonable to assume that the applicant is available for immediate employment. However, an availability date in the future need not be a strike against an applicant. For many reasons (vacation, clean up loose ends), some applicants may prefer a break between jobs, and some managers feel that a person who leaves "personal space" between jobs is one who has his priorities straight and is apt to be a better adjusted employee.

CONCLUSION

From the applicant's side, a resume should not be seen as an immediate ticket to a good job. But it is an entree, a way to attract an employer's attention, a way to highlight skills, experiences, and goals.

From the employer's side, a resume should never be used as the sole basis for making a "hire/not hire" decision. It can be a useful way to do a first selection, and it can point out areas for further discusion with the candidate.

Read between the lines of every resume. Review the article on resume preparation in the Appendix of this book to get a feel for the advice resume writers get. Remain alert to questions, issues, and insights that any resume generates, and plan to follow through with the applicant in a personal interview.

4
General
Interviewing Skills

M anagers get involved in many different kinds of interviews: employment interviews, job performance interviews, and promotion interviews, among others. Yet many managers who enjoy people and are good communicators in general feel nervous about this particular one-to-one communication.

This may be because an interview is a *formal* communication that differs from spontaneous everyday communication. Although no two interviews are alike in their nature and content, they all share several important structural similarities: the interviewer is looking for specific information from the interviewee. At the same time, the interviewer wishes to put the interviewee at ease and to maintain his own positive self-image. Special skills are vital to keeping the interview on track and maximizing the flow of information.

These skills are not innate. Good interviews are made and refined, not born. Interviewing and listening techniques can be learned.

Applying active listening and interviewing techniques will help promote you as a person who cares about people as individuals. It will improve communications with your present and prospective employees. And it will help produce the kind of information you need as a manager.

HEARING, LISTENING, AND INTERVIEWING

An effective interviewer requires three basic skills.[1] He must have considerable knowledge of the subject or topic being discussed in the interview. He must be able to form appropriate questions that will draw out of the other person the information required. And, the effective interviewer must be an active listener.

A major difficulty managers have with interviewing is that they take for granted the act of listening. They confuse listening with hearing and assume that listening requires no practice or effort. Hearing is *not* listening. Hearing is such a common activity that we forget it is happening, and we assume that listening takes no effort.

If a person's hearing is impaired, mechanical devices can often restore some of the lost hearing ability.

Hearing is mechanical, and because it happens with no apparent effort on our part, we assume that when a listening failure occurs, it is the other person's fault.

FAULT OF THE SENDER

When listening is interrupted, or when a miscommunication occurs, most of us are quick to blame the sender. His voice was not loud enough. Her ideas were poorly presented. They spoke too fast, or too slow, or too long, or not long enough. Hearing the words spoken, even making sense of the words being said, is not listening.

ACTIVE LISTENING

Listening is an active process. It involves understanding the meanings of words, expressions, and ideas and evaluating the content of the message. It requires the listener to assimilate, or make a part of himself, the message or the thought being sent. Each of these processes—understanding, evaluating, assimilating—requires the conscious action of the listener.

Human relations experts have frequently suggested that the greatest barrier to people understanding people is our basic inability to actively listen to others. In the words of another manager, "Everyone has learned to talk, but no one has learned to listen."

LISTENING HABITS

Habits are actions that are performed without thinking. When you brush your teeth, or say thank you, or even breathe, you do it out of habit. Habits are developed by consciously doing something over and over again, until your mind no longer needs a conscious signal to perform. Some of our habits are good—they cause us to take beneficial or profitable actions. Other habits are not so good, leading us to unthinkingly do things that are harmful, or unproductive, or stupid.

Good listening results from careful cultivation of positive listening activities. Although listening is an active process, it need not be a completely conscious one. The secret to better listening is to develop good listening habits.[2]

A CONVERSATION OR A SPEECH?

Most of the important aspects of good listening apply to a formal speech situation as well as a quiet conversation between a manager and an employee. Some listening problems happen more often in a large group while one person is talking, and other problems are more commonly found when two or three individuals communicate face-to-face. By developing good listening habits, you can overcome many communication difficulties that plague management. These same good habits of listening can add measurably to the quantity *and* quality of information available to you as you work to meet your managerial responsibilities.

Earlier we suggested that the habits we form have a powerful and long-lasting effect on our communicative behavior. Some of these habits are productive and help us communicate better. Other habits are bad habits, and they keep us from fully developing our communication skills. In listening, bad habits are developed from years of experience, and they can cause us to distort and miss messages that we ought to get. Since we assume that some listeners have some bad listening habits, let's look at how these bad habits can be reversed to produce some good listening habits or practices.

Concentrate on the Speaker's Strength

Few people are blessed with the winning combination of a good delivery and an interesting, stimulating subject. When either the subject or the speaker is dull, we often find it easy to tune out and then blame the speaker for our listening failure. Some of the blame for listening failure is the fault of the speaker.

However, this should not bother the good listener. The good listener has developed the habit of focusing her attention on the key aspects of a presentation, either in a two-person conversation or a large-audience lecture.

If the speaker is dull, repetitive, or if he speaks in a monotone, the good listener doesn't tune out. Instead he works harder to focus more attention on the subject being discussed. No matter what the subject, there are at least one or two facts (or at least some inferences) that can be extracted and used. The active listener works at finding and evaluating those facts and inferences.

If the subject is dull, boring, totally irrelevant, and beyond salvation, the good listener focuses on the speaker's delivery. How does she pronounce words? What does her voice accent say about where she grew up? By observing people, the good listener is able to turn an otherwise wasted time into some beneficial outcome.

But what if both speaker *and* subject are dull, boring, etc? As a last resort, the good listener may turn his attention to the reactions of the audience. What body postures or facial expressions indicate how they feel about the experience?

Perhaps we are stretching things a bit too far. Still, active listening implies a conscious strategy to understand, evaluate, and assimilate and to profit personally from any listening situation. Assuming you have no choice *but* to stay and endure, why not make the best of it? With this attitude, no situation, however bleak, is a total "listening loss." Positive listening habits can be a good defense against boredom and fatigue.

Stay Cool

Often, while we're listening, a word or a phrase or an expression can trigger an emotional reaction. We get overstimulated and immediately block out whatever else is said.

Good listeners develop the habit of staying cool when an emotional situation develops. No one is immune to emotion, but the good listener has a habit of recognizing the emotional trigger and neutralizing it *before* it blocks the rest of the message. This requires concentration and the ability to move your attention quickly.

Often, emotional words come into a conversation (although rarely in a speech) from some racial or ethnic prejudice. A Polish sales manager would "see red" every time a certain ethnic slur made its way into a conversation either by mistake or on purpose. Knowing his hatred for such a slur, two of his employees delighted in upsetting their boss whenever his discomfort would help them reach their goals. His "lack of cool" became a major barrier to his listening skills. The sales manager missed many important ideas and bits of information in meetings, simply because he was unable to overcome his listening defect.

No one likes to be insulted, and such insults are usually a display of a speaker's ignorance. Managers who habitually use such expressions run a great risk of blocking the listening of others around them. (Not to mention their alienation and distrust.) However, managers who fail to recognize the effects of such emotional words on their own listening ability are likely to encounter more problems as they go.

Many police experts realize the damaging effects of emotional words on the behavior of officers. Police reaction to demonstrators of the 1960s was often linked to an involuntary reaction to taunts and insults. Racial or ethnic slurs, shouts of "pigs" and other obscenities caused a temporary blocking of rational thought processes. To combat such reactions, police departments instituted "sensitivity training." Such training is credited by many experts with helping police under verbal fire to retain their cool and to perform their jobs in the usual professional manner.

Sensitivity training is not universally accepted as a means of overcoming listening blocks. It can, however, give you an insight into your own pattern of biases. Next time you're listening to a speech or engaged in conversation with an employee, watch for words or expressions that raise your pulse or breathing or cause you to lose track of your thoughts. Knowing what turns you off can be important in keeping your listening ability turned on.

Overstimulation

Another bad habit of listening is closely related to emotional words because it causes a similar reaction. In a meeting or discussion, a controversial or provocative idea may pop into your head. Whether the idea is a good one or a bad one, the usual reaction will still be the same. The poor listener immediately starts making mental or written notes about the idea and ignoring what the speaker says next. This isn't as much of a problem if you're tape-recording the conversation. You can let your mind wander and get the speaker's other points later. However, the tape lacks the speaker's body communication, which can be a major portion of his total message. Even taping may not overcome all the problems, but without such a backup, you risk losing important information.

Don't Think About Elephants!

Whatever you do, don't think about elephants!

Now—what's on your mind? Either you're thinking about elephants or you're trying very hard to *not* think about elephants. Either way, you're distracted from what you want to do.

Causing a distraction is rude. There is little excuse for doing so. But, too often, tolerating a distraction can be just as damaging to your powers of listening as the actual distraction itself. Since many people can't control where or when a conversation with an employee will take place, they're at the mercy of all sorts of distractions—loud noise, others present within earshot, ringing phones, etc. Trying to overcome these distractions by tolerating them can lead to some unfortunate consequences.

A young supervisor with General Motors had many opportunities to participate in staff meetings. The boss was a hardworking, capable manager whose philosophy of management included a minimum number of meetings. When he did call a meeting, everyone of his employees knew that what he said would be important. There was plenty of motivation for good, active listening.

The boss had one disturbing habit. Every time he'd get up to talk, his hand would rattle the coins in his pocket. This was a distraction, and everyone in the meetings knew it. To compensate, everyone worked very hard to overlook the obvious distraction. In fact, they tried too hard. Instead of being distracted by the jingling coins, they were distracted by the act of *tolerating the distraction*.

Good listeners who face distraction must walk a delicate balance. They must overlook the distraction itself while not getting too wrapped up in tolerating it. When distractions do occur, try concentrating your attention in a positive way on the ideas of the other person is giving you. In this way, the distraction is minimized without the need for toleration.

Just the Facts, Nothing but the Facts

Everyone takes justifiable pride in being able to size up people and potential in a factual, objective way. Too much subjectivity, we've been told, leads to ill feelings, poor communications, and inefficiency in management.

Yet listening only for facts is a filtering process that can be a source of noise or distortion. To learn more about a person or a situation, we must become more sensitive to the *context* as well as the actual facts. Much can be learned from attitudes, feelings, and inferences. Blocking or filtering them out is a bad listening habit.

A good listener overcomes the "inference-observation" confusion by correctly labeling and using both kinds of information. Obviously, feelings and inferences alone are usually a poor guide to action. But so are facts alone.

Good, active listeners make lists, either on paper or in their heads. One list is titled "fact," a second "feelings/attitudes of the speaker," and perhaps a third is labeled "how *I* feel about what the speaker said." Doing so accomplishes a number of good results. It helps a listener to avoid getting trapped with incomplete information. It correctly labels information for future use. It also helps you to make sense out of a speaker whose remarks are not presented according to some outline.

Outline Everything

In school, we're taught to make an outline before writing or speaking. An outline helps organize thoughts in a logical manner and prevents confusion and rambling. There's no question about the importance of an outline to a sender.

However, most conversations and many formal presentations have no outline. Instead, the speaker simply says whatever pops into his mind. The words spoken may or may not be related to the subject being discussed. Trying to put those kinds of remarks into a neat academic outline simply won't work.

Good listeners know this and avoid consciously trying to shoehorn everything into an outline. Instead, they use the three-column method for mental or written notes. If a speaker in a formal presentation is speaking from an outline, the notes you take will look like an outline. If not, your notes will still be well organized. You will have the best chance for coming away from the presentation or conversation with usable, meaningful information.

Suppose a production run was ruined because of incorrect material specifications. That fact is more useful to you in making later decisions if you are also aware that your lead worker was suspicious of the specifications in the first place. The opinions plus the facts can prevent a similar failure in the future. Facts alone may cause you to "reinvent the wheel," and make the same error again.

The Listening Posture

Most of us can remember parents or other adults telling us, "Sit up and pay attention when I'm talking to you!" A listening posture is important to the talker as well as the listener. If you slouch in your chair or let your eyes wander while someone is talking to you, you may give them the impression that you don't care for their ideas or their needs. You'll give negative body signals that may seriously damage communication. Using your body language to encourage the speaker is a good strategy for improving communication, especially in small group conversations and discussions. (In Chapter 14, we'll discuss in much more detail how you can use your body language as a positive management tool.)

There is also a negative side to taking a "listening posture." Too often, we prepare to listen by sitting erect, eyes forward, arms folded on the chest or resting on the table, and chin up. Once this posture is assumed, we are then absolved from any blame if a communication failure does occur. Having taken a listening posture, the poor listener assumes that there is *no way* to keep from listening.

This attitude reflects the confusion between hearing and listening. As we've said, hearing is a physical activity. Taking a listening posture can help your ability to hear better, but hearing is not listening, and listening is mental activity. It requires conscious and continuous activity.

Test yourself. The next time you are in a meeting, ask yourself if you are assuming too much by simply sitting in a listening position. Chances are, you find your mind wandering even though you feel mentally comfortable because you *think* you're listening.

Teachers and managers know that students and employees seem to be able to sleep with their eyes open. Don't fall into the bad habit of assuming that your physical posture *automatically* keeps you actively listening.

Reading the Funnies

Managers often find themselves in a listening rut because they listen to the same kinds of people with the same problems day after day. They don't take (or make) opportunities to challenge and improve their listening skills. If you never read anything more challenging than the Sunday funnies your ability to read will never grow beyond the funnies. The same is true of listening.

A common bad habit of listening is to listen only to familiar ideas and familiar people in familiar surroundings. This sameness quickly results in a severely limited ability to listen to (and understand) more complex and complicated ideas.

Good listeners challenge themselves regularly. A Texas supervisor in an airport maintenance shop regularly sits in on public lectures at a local community college. He admits that many of the speakers and their presentations are way over his head. He also believes that this challenge helps keep his listening ability sharp and prevents what he calls mental rusting. You're no farther away from listening challenges than your home television. All networks (especially the Public Television Network) regularly present speakers and topics that challenge your listening ability. You don't have to agree with the speaker or share his viewpoint. You gain as an active listener by simply exposing yourself to a listening challenge and by working to take even one new idea from a difficult presentation. Managers who work in a bilingual or multilingual environment can use television for another listening exercise. English-speaking managers report much improved communication with their French- or Spanish-speaking employees when they (the managers) develop the habit of watching some television programs broadcast in the "foreign" language. Try it. You may not actually learn a new language, but you will gain a better understanding of your non-English speaking employees. By tuning in to Spanish-accented or French-accented speaking, your listening skills will be profitably improved.

Why Do We Daydream?

Have you ever found yourself in a listening situation where your mind began to wander? For each of us, daydreaming is a common activity. Listening experts tell us that part of the reason we daydream or wander while we're supposed to be listening is that our mind works faster than most talkers can talk. Most people speak about 125 words per minute in normal conversation. Yet the average mind is able to listen to and comprehend as many as four hundred words per minute. The wide difference between speaking and listening rates gives us plenty of time for daydreams.

Bad listeners have a habit of wasting this additional listening power. In contrast, good listeners use the speed differential to review what the speaker has already said and to anticipate where the speaker is going.

Correcting Our Bad Habits

We've examined several habits that contribute to poor listening. For each bad habit, there is a corrective, a good habit to help make you a better listener. Let's summarize by looking at three positive strategies for becoming an active listener.

1. Anticipate the next point and how you'll respond to it.
2. Break down a conversation into its main and supporting elements.
3. Make periodic mental summaries, and assure yourself that you're on the same track as the person you are interviewing.

LISTENING TECHNIQUES

From years of psychoanalytical and psychological study of human behavior, experts have learned much that can be helpful in improving our listening skills. We shall now discuss some very useful and practical techniques for *all* listening situations.

Patience

When you're listening, let the other person finish what she is trying to say. Many people have great difficulty putting their thoughts and ideas into words. They pause, stammer, and repeat while trying to find the right words. If you try to rush them or finish the thought before the sentence is complete, you'll only succeed in causing more hesitation, more uncertainty. Even if you believe that what you're being told is wrong (or irrelevant), give the speaker a chance at self-expression. You can help overcome reluctance or insecurity by giving simple signs of acceptance. These signs do not have to mean that you agree with the speaker, only that you are listening with interest and understanding.

Give Encouraging Gestures

Be mindful of the powerful impact of your nonverbal messages. Your posture, facial expression, hand gestures, and voice cues all transmit messages to the person speaking. You can communicate disinterest or hostility by avoiding eye contact, or by keeping your arms tightly crossed over your chest and your body turned away from the other person. Gestures can also be approving or encouraging. They can help put the prospective employee at ease and promote more open and honest communication. Try to maintain frequent eye contact without staring or "looking through" the other person. Lean forward and keep your facial expression open and direct. Watch for opportunities to nod or murmur "I see" or "um-hm." None of these gestures need signify agreement, only interest and concern.

Listen for Feelings

Often, the most important things to listen for are the feelings and attitudes of the speaker. Even if a person is good at reporting facts or describing events, he may be unable to adequately express his needs, desires, and feelings. Careful attention to such detail is essential. As you listen, restate the other person's thought or feeling. With a brief but accurate restatement, you act as a mirror. You encourage your speaker to continue talking while you demonstrate your interest in his thoughts. Such comments as "you say Joe seems to be the cause?," or "you feel you're ready to be reconsidered?" don't have to imply anything on your part. Such statements simply help maintain a neutral listening environment.

You can use the same device to get more facts. Simply add a question mark to your voice as you restate the other person's thought. For example, if she says that she feels your project is in trouble, you can respond by saying, "the project is in trouble?" With this encouragement, she may amplify her statement and bring up some new facts, objections, or opinions. You can then make a more intelligent and informed response to those facts, objections, or opinions.

Because feelings are delicate and easily turned off, try to avoid direct or "threatening statements," at least until you have a firm grasp of the situation *as the speaker sees it.* Such comments as "You're wrong," "Hold on a minute, look at the facts," or "I don't believe you" can quickly put the speaker into a defensive (and less communicative) mood. Even if you know the speaker is wrong (or worse, lying), try to keep your verbal responses and body expressions neutral for as long as possible. Later, you may want to take the offensive and probe areas where contradictions appear. However, as long as the speaker volunteers information, and as long as that information is relevant to solving a problem, challenging the speaker can be unproductive.

What You Don't Say

Listen for what the speaker is saying, and listen also for what the speaker is not saying. If particular parts of a subject or problem are being omitted even after some encouragement from you, it may indicate that the subject is delicate. That may be the clue to solving a problem. Many of us cover up our reluctance to discuss certain facts by using too many cliché terms, or by repeating facts already mentioned. Develop a sensitivity to clichés and contents and to obvious evasions or omissions. They may be important clues.

A polygraph (lie detector) is designed to measure very small changes in heartbeat, skin temperature, and dryness. The machines work on the assumption that there is a direct relationship between these changes and a person's conscious attempts to avoid the truth. As an active listener, you can use this concept to your advantage. Watch for hand gestures (gripping tightly, sweaty palms), excessive eye contact, or squirming in the chair. These and other signals may tip you off to a lie or an evasion of important facts. Naturally, you can't be as sensitive or accurate as a polygraph, but you can measurably improve your ability to read signals.

Watch the Great "I"

Beware of too much direct personal involvement, especially in the early stages of a conversation. If the speaker really wants to hear your thoughts or opinion, give an honest reply. Too much evasion on your part can be damaging. There is, of course, no rule that applies in all cases. Wherever possible during a listening encounter, reflect the speaker's views and try to avoid a direct statement of personal views. Often, managers find that employees ask for their opinion in order to know what things are appropriate to discuss. "Reading the boss" may be useful to an employee, but it can seriously hamper identification of problems.

It is a common human emotion to like being told what we want to hear. However, when prospective employees play "guess what you're thinking," good communication suffers. By keeping your opinions and ideas out of a sales conversation, you encourage free and more open communication.

Along with holding back personal views (or those of his organization), a good listener also avoids getting himself emotionally involved. Too much emotion is a bad habit because it can quickly pull the listening encounter away from where it ought to be.

Allow Time

Nothing subverts good managerial communication more than interruptions. When you are talking or listening to an employee, try to find a time and place where your conversation can continue uninterrupted. Even when the subject under discussion is impersonal or unimportant, an employee will quickly lose track of his thoughts when other people pop in unexpectedly or when the telephone rings. A good listening setting is one where people communicating are free from unnecessary interruption.

NO "ONE BEST WAY" TO INTERVIEW

A single common interviewing style won't work in all situations simply because no two people are exactly alike. For example, some scientific or engineering people may be comfortable with facts and data—they have little difficulty elaborating on financial or technical information. These same people may feel uncomfortable talking about themselves.

Some people may be threatened by the appearance and physical setting of the interviewer's office or interview room and respond poorly to direct or technical questions. The successful interviewer is one who can adapt both to the experienced interviewee and the less sophisticated individual who may be in her first interview.

We use our own jargon when communicating. Jargon makes us feel comfortable and can be an efficient means of communicating within an organization. However, using jargon with outsiders creates barriers. Successful adaptation often means talking in the interviewee's own "language."

The key to successful adaptation is to respond to the interviewee. The successful interviewer is a person who can change her style as an interview develops so that information can be obtained in the least threatening way.

The "You" View

A common problem interviewers face is the difficulty of presenting information from the interviewee's point of view. In learning to adapt your interviewing style, you can use the "you" view. A "you viewpoint" involves presenting ideas from the listener's or interviewee's point of view rather than from the interviewer's point of view. For example:

(We): "We will process your application."
(You): "Your application will be processed."
(We): "Our employee standards are designed to protect the institution."
(You): "The employee standards you'll work with benefit you by making your job easier and your work more productive."

In these examples, notice how the "me" or "we" viewpoint contrasts with the "you" viewpoint. Similar information is communicated, but the "you" viewpoint helps the interviewee relate to it more easily and effectively.

Taking a "you" viewpoint is an extension of your interviewer role as a counselor. Since a counselor should deal with people in a positive and helpful way, the "you" view helps create good will and helps the interviewee relax and communicate more freely.

Get an Answer, Not Just a Response

When you meet a person in the morning, the conversation usually sounds something like: "Good morning, how are you today?" "Fine, how are you?" "See you later." The contacts or transactions involve questions that don't really require answers. In fact, we'd be rather embarrassed or upset if someone did respond to our question, "How are you today?" with a detailed account of their Saturday-night date, their last operation, or the current state of their love or financial affairs.

Asking "How are you today?" is a rhetorical question requiring only a response. Such conversational questions are devices that don't call for an answer or any deeper level of interpersonal involvement. However, in an interview, it is the responsibility of the interviewer to get answers to questions, not just responses.

Because of fear or uncertainty, an interviewee may try to "read" you and respond to your questions with answers that he feels you really want. This results in "phony feedback," and can be very unproductive. Since answers are important, let's examine how an interview should be conducted to maximize the amount of useful information obtained and to minimize phony feedback.

Opening the Interview

The opening of an interview is critical. Properly done, it can help remove some of the jitters and nervousness that most people feel when being interviewed. To put your interviewee at ease, open an interview by building rapport between you and the other person. This reduces defensiveness and helps establish good will.

Building rapport is a skill. It requires a sensitivity to the interviewee's needs. The challenge is to open the lines of communication in a way that doesn't condescend or put the interviewee in an obvious "put-down" position. You can build rapport in many ways. Good listening is important. As the conversation opens, you should stay somewhat in the background while getting acquainted takes place. Lean forward and keep a direct "eye-lock" on the interviewee—which communicates warmth and personal concern.

At the same time, reduce defensiveness by removing some of the barriers between you and your interviewee. Because of the perceived pressure in an interview, people being interviewed tend to sit as far as possible from an interviewer, on the opposite side of the desk, even leaning back in their chairs. To combat this defensiveness, invite interviewees to sit at the side of your desk. Lean forward, arms away from your body, eyes making contact, with a warm, expansive smile that says, "I'm not here to threaten you. I want to solve a problem and you can help."

Rapport can also be established by briefly asking the interviewee about himself in a nonthreatening way. Ask about hobbies, children, interests, and other pursuits. These are subjects people are willing to talk about freely.

Environmental factors, too, play an important part in the formation of attitudes. For example, in Figure 3, assume you as the interviewer are sitting in position number 1.

Looking at the other positions around your desk, where would

FIGURE 3.

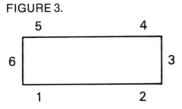

you put the other person to make her comfortable? You'll usually find that the position arrangement 1-5 is the most competitive arrangement. Two people sitting on opposite sides of a desk or some other fixed barrier facing each other directly with no angles between their bodies will probably feel competitive.

Although this arrangement isn't necessarily bad in an interview, it's not the best arrangement for developing cooperation and open communication. On the other hand, the most cooperative position arrangement would be 1-6, where the two parties sit with some angles in their body positions (rather than face-to-face) and where they have the opportunity to look at each other face-to-face or look away at the desk without threatening each other with the loss of eye contact.

In the 1-6 position, you're more likely to feel cooperative, and you're more likely to create rapport than in the competitive 1-5 position. An important part of the 1-6 arrangement is a reduction in the amount of desk between the participants. As more and more desk is removed, the two persons come closer together. More important, the psychological barrier is also reduced.

However, don't automatically assume that removing desk barriers creates greater rapport. In the 1-2 position, where there is no desk between the two parties, the physical barriers are gone, but discomfort is likely to be high. Most of us like some protection between ourselves and others. The 1-2 position doesn't provide it. Both parties are face-to-face and body to body, with nothing separating them. This can cause uneasiness.

Another important aspect of nonverbal communication in interviewing is privacy. Many studies of interpersonal space and its effect on behavior and attitude show that an interviewee's comfort and willingness to communicate directly relate to the amount of privacy he is given during the interview. When an interview takes place in an open area with other desks, and when other conversations are going on simultaneously, a person is apt to feel threatened and is less likely to open up in a frank, honest way.

On the other hand, when interviews are conducted in private ceiling-to-floor walled offices with closed doors, people will be more communicative. They feel a greater sense of comfort knowing that their ideas and feelings will be kept private. The problem is not one of actual privacy, but rather of perceived privacy. Even half walls separating the desks of interviewers contribute to a perceived sense of privacy, although there is no difference in the actual privacy when half-wall arrangements are compared with no-barriers arrangements.

You may not be able to control the setting in which you conduct interviews themselves, but you can influence the arrangement of your immediate work area. For example, by moving chairs closer to your desk, your interview can create a much more isolated or "private space" for interviewing.

The opening of the interview is the appropriate time for such issues of space and interpersonal distance to be settled. It does little good to begin an interview at a formal distance and then to invite the interviewee to move in closer; this signal may be perceived as manipulative or threatening. However, since many interviews open with the interviewer and interviewee in a standing position shaking hands, the interviewer can then direct the interviewee to sit in a particular chair. This way, it's possible to control the physical arrangement of an interview right from the time it begins.

Also, watch how you shake hands. Whenever possible, shake hands without crossing over the width of the desk. A handshake should take place at the side or front of the desk, with the interviewer stepping forward to greet the interviewee. Shaking hands over a desk can create additional barriers. It calls attention to the difference between the roles of the interviewer and interviewee and becomes a potential barrier.

Use Understandable Language

When conducting an interview, your language should be adapted to the language and the needs of the interviewee. People exposed to unfamiliar jargon rarely ask for definitions. They pretend to understand and thus risk making serious errors.

Interviewers should be sure their purpose is clear in their own minds before conducting an interview. Remember that in face-to-face communication an interviewer should use language that will help to express what she is thinking rather than to impress the interviewee. Common words should be used whenever possible, and the words that are used should express in the simplest possible way what the interviewer is trying to say.

In most financial circles the word *escheat* is defined as "money which is held on account but which can't be spent." It is also used in some financial institutions to indicate a deficiency in an account. A woman called her credit union asking why her share drafts were "bounced." She was told that her share account had been escheated. Very indignantly, she said, "You're darn right you've escheated my account and I want it stopped immediately!" Her misunderstanding of the word *escheat* didn't prevent her from venting her feelings about having it done to her account.

Good word choice requires a certain amount of sensitivity on the part of the interviewer. When discussing technical terms with interviewees, interviewers should avoid such phrases as "you know that" or "everyone knows that" or "as you already are aware" followed by a definition. This suggests that "even though I'm asking you to indicate that you already know the answer, I'm not sure you are smart enough to really know it. Therefore, I will tell you the answer to the puzzle." Offer definitions in a matter-of-fact way, as though the definition is an integral part of your language. The interviewee won't feel as threatened, since he can stop the defining by saying "I do understand" rather than being put down.

Use Positive Words

In an interview, positive words should be used whenever possible. Positive words create good will. Positive words are more likely to persuade and to convince the interviewee, if that is the purpose of the interview. It is also important for the interviewer to avoid negative words, or words that carry a connotation of negativity. For example: Rather than, "Your application can't be accepted unless you complete all items," say, "Your application will be accepted when all items are complete."

The Funnel Approach to Questioning

An important tool in planning and executing a good interview is use of the funnel approach. This involves moving through an interview from general topics to specific topics.

Focusing on general topics at the opening of an interview helps put the interviewee at ease. People feel more comfortable talking about themselves in a general and unthreatening way.

By moving from the general to the specific, it is also possible for an interviewer to spot potential trouble areas where more intensive questioning may be necessary.

By allowing people in the early stages of the interview to choose their own topics and discuss in their own words what they feel important, an interviewer may learn important information.

An example of the funnel principle is the problem of using yes/no responses to determine which card a person has chosen from an ordinary deck of cards. In this game, we assume that the only answer you will be given is yes or no. How many questions must you ask before you can identify the card the other person has chosen?

The first two questions might be: (1) "Is the card you are holding black?'' (2) ''Is the card you are holding a spade?'' Or, if the response was red, ''Is the card you are holding a heart?'' From these two questions it should be possible to identify the suit of the chosen card. Question 3 might be, ''Is the card you are holding a picture card?'' The next question (4) narrows still further. ''Is the card you are holding a Jack or Queen?'' or ''Is the card you are holding a six or below?''

As you become more specific, you should be able to identify the chosen card in six questions, if the questions are phrased carefully and if a funnel approach is followed. In the same way, a logical approach to picking up on signals in the early stages of an interview can make the interviewer's job much easier when specific and difficult questions are asked in the latter part of the interview. Notice in our example that the first question narrows the possible cards from 52 to 26 possibilities. As the questions become more and more specific, the number of possible answers represented continues to decrease until you reach the correct answer.

Contrast the funnel approach in an effective interview with the kind of questioning used in presidential news conferences. Invariably, such news conferences are under the total control of the president. Since the administration of John Kennedy, to the consternation and constant complaint of the news media, presidents have used press conferences as a device for reaching their own goals.

Yet the questioning conducted by the news people is disjointed, with very little follow-up from one question to the next, and as a result of such random questioning, the president is in full control of the ''interview.''

In a business interview, it would be unproductive to permit the interviewee to maintain such control. Therefore, the questioning must be much more structured and must be aimed at specific informational objectives.

Consider the funnel approach applied to a job-filling interview. The general question should be asked first, and ideally it should be an open-minded question: ''Tell me about yourself.'' The next question can be a direct question: ''What jobs have you had in the past?'' We have in two questions given the interviewee the opportunity to say whatever she feels is important about her personal history.

A third question may be either a specific question or a closed question such as ''Why do you want this job?'' Another question that is appropriate at this point might be a yes/no question, such as ''Have you ever worked with MCT-type systems?'' If the answer is no, other lines of questioning are then appropriate. If the answer is yes, further specific questioning on the subject may be appropriate. Such questions may focus on related issues such as prior training, prior experience, or other matters related to previous work history.

The final questions (at the bottom of the funnel) should be probing questions, dealing with specific kinds of information.

In-Depth Questioning

Once you have put an interviewee at ease and have determined the approach you will take, you are ready for the real heart of the interview—the in-depth questioning. The ultimate success of the meeting or interview will be dependent on the types of questions asked that will ferret out specific information needed for drawing the right conclusions.

There are serveral reasons why an interviewer should ask probing questions. One of the most important reasons is to get some elaboration on matters that may have emerged earlier in the "general" part of the interview. This elaboration may be to achieve additional insight into information that may have surfaced in a tangential way. Elaboration questions include "What else?" or "What other reasons?" or "Tell me more about _____."

These questions clearly put the burden on the interviewee to elaborate, although they need not be framed in a threatening way. Rather they should be expressed as a simple desire of the interviewer to learn more. Such questions should refer to the fact that the interviewee has himself raised the issue that is now being probed. As such, elaboration questions can be prefaced, "You mentioned earlier something about your troubles with Mr. Metavish in data processing. What do you feel are the reasons for these troubles?" Suggest to the interviewee that he is being cooperative and that you would like more elaboration on a point he has already raised.

However, some elaboration questions must be posed on matters that the interviewee has never raised. In the probing questions, the interviewer should never avoid silence. Waiting for an answer puts pressure on the interviewee to reply with something more than just a response. When a simple yes/no response is given, don't accept such a response. Probe further for an answer. Restate your question by asking it in a different way.

Maintain eye contact with the interviewee, even after a yes/no or otherwise unresponsive answer. Silence will force the interviewee into making additional elaborations. This may lead to new information you did not anticipate and can give new insights into the interviewee's thinking.

Car dealers use this "silent treatment" to appraise cars being traded for newer models. A cheap paint job and heavy oil can often disguise many auto ills found in older-model cars, and direct questions about previous ownership, accidents, and repairs may result in uninformative responses. Clever salespeople and appraisers know that silence, eye contact, and a friendly but inquiring manner lead to information that might not be obtained in any other way. Since some information can be quite sensitive, it's wise to apply this interviewing device of the professional appraiser.

Use probing questions for clarification. The purpose of clarifying questions is to have the interviewee explain herself through answering such questions as "What do you mean by that?" or "How do you mean that?"

Use probing questions to maintain the relevance of the interview. In a conversation, it's easy to get off track. In a conversation, that is no real problem, but in an interview it can be. Probing and clarifying questions help keep the interviewee dealing with a particular issue instead of moving away to more comfortable or familiar ground. An example of a probing question is "let me restate this" or "let me see if I understand what you are saying" followed by a brief restatement of where the interview was before it began to move off the track.

Use probing questions to appraise the validity of the information received. Although probing questions may be used to determine if the respondent is being honest, successful interviewers also match responses with the speaker's body language. For example, persons who are lying often avoid direct eye contact.

However, as we become more sophisticated, body language observers suggest that eye contact alone is no longer a clear way to determine if an individual is lying, since many people have become adept at lying while using good eye contact. For this reason, combine analysis of eye contact with analysis of quivering voice, jittering or fidgeting in the seat, all of which may be signs that the respondent is nervous, upset, ill at ease, or lying. In the early stages of an interview, such signals may simply result from fear, misunderstanding, and perceived threat. In general, the nonverbal clues to one's attitudes are better indicators of one's true intent or meaning than are one's verbal messages, simply because nonverbal signals are constantly and subconsciously being transmitted.

Feet can be an important credibility verifier. Even if a person is conscious of his eye contact, hand grip, and body movement, he will seldom pay much attention to how he holds or moves his feet. For example, a person being interviewed about his employment background is likely to feel considerable pressure to put up a good front. If he knows the potential for body communication, he will probably keep his hands still and his eyes comfortably level with yours. Watch his feet. Frequently crossing and uncrossing legs or rapidly tapping or shaking the foot are all potential signals that the person is nervous. More important, changes in these signals (moving, shaking, or recrossing faster than usual) may indicate particularly sensitive subjects you may want to pursue in more depth. The important point here is to be sensitive to more body messages than just the "standard eye-hand" combinations.

The Mirror Question

The mirror question is another interesting device for interviews. It involves restating a person's last comment as a question. For example, if the interviewee suggests, "I haven't had any real difficulty," the interviewer may respond with a raised eyebrow and the statement, "You say you haven't had recent difficulties?" The respondent is thus told, "I am a little suspicious of your statement" and "I would like more clarification and information on that statement."

Mirror questions are also validating questions, since they permit the interviewer to ask the same question over and over again in different ways under the guise of turning back on a person the answers he has given to a previous question.

The Leading Question

Leading questions are interesting, since they require taking an aggressive stance. Leading questions can encourage the interviewee to develop some commitment to a program or plan that evolves from an interview. Questions such as "Don't you agree that . . .?" or "You are aware of the surcharge, aren't you?" are leading questions.

In an interview, one type of question to avoid is the leading question that puts the interviewee in a double bind. For example: "Have you stopped beating. . . .?" gives the respondent no acceptable way to respond. As a result, leading questions cause resentment or hostility and may actually result in less information than one might expect. The best examples of leading questions were those from a state legislator in his constituent newsletter. He asked for their opinion with the following questions.

1. Should the State violate the laws of God, nature, and man and legalize murder by abortion?
2. Should the State enact the Gestapo law and encourage people to spy on their neighbors by reporting such minor violations as air and water pollution?

Such questions are designed to lead the respondent in a particular direction. Although there is no real harm in asking a leading question, the results will invariably be unsatisfactory. When you ask such a question, you get phony feedback. People tell you just what you want to hear—because you have set them up.

Keep Sight of Your Priorities

In an interview, keep sight of your objective. Interviewers tend to lose sight of the fact that the main purpose of the interview is to gain information from the interviewee. An interview is not the time or place for dazzling displays of wit or random expertise. Neither should an interview take on an air of "interrogation," which can lead to defensiveness.

By keeping your primary objectives in mind, you can be supportive, creating a comfortable yet businesslike atmosphere that will result in the maximum amount of information being obtained in the minimum amount of time.

The Bad-News Message

One important concern in interviewing is the situation where people must be turned down or rejected. "Bad-news" situations make most of us uncomfortable. As a result, we mishandle many of them. While we are thinking about face-to-face interviews, we can learn a lot about giving bad news from the way bad-news letters are written.

In a bad-news letter, the bad news is apt to put the receiver in a poor frame of mind. The letter writer must convey the bad-news message without further antagonizing the receiver. This means sending the bad news while maintaining whatever good will it is possible to maintain with the receiver.

In a bad-news interview, it is best to take an indirect approach. Using a slower pace and emphasizing the positive at the beginning and end of the interview can help overcome some of the negative effects of the bad news. This is the "sandwich effect," with the bad news sandwiched between good news. For example: Suppose a person's request for a transfer must be turned down. This is bad news, since the new job is what the person wants and cannot have. Assuming that you want the employee to remain motivated and productive, you should give the message in a way that minimizes negative effects.

As you begin the interview, briefly outline some of the employee's strengths. Point out some of the features of her work profile that may make this individual a sound prospect for future promotion or transfer consideration. The bad news can then be given using the "you" viewpoint. This will help the employee understand the reasons for the turndown, from her point of view. The interview can then be closed on a more constructive note.

There are problems with using a sandwich approach for presenting bad news. Many people want to get their bad news directly. Because you feel capable of handling personal bad news without the sandwich, you may want to treat everyone the same way. However, psychological studies show that when bad news must be delivered, the sandwich approach is the most productive and humane way to do so. The message is more understandable and acceptable.

Often, in an attempt to develop empathy between ourselves and the interviewee, we explain negative decisions or bad news by suggesting that something is "against company policy." In effect, company policy prevents a positive decision. Although this approach may be useful in creating empathy, it does nothing to help the rejected person see things from his own point of view.

Policy statements are not "you-viewpoint" statements. They are "me" or "we" viewpoint statements, reflecting only the wishes and problems of the person talking. Instead of the "policy, sorry" technique, use the common-goal technique.

Common Goal

The common-goal technique puts you in a counselor role. For example, "we wouldn't want you transferred to where you'll be unhappy." As part of your counselor role, emphasize the common goals of employee satisfaction and company productivity. In effect, "We cannot grant your request now, but with continued experience and training, you'll be in a better position in the future to get the position and responsibilities you want."

With a common-goal approach, you develop a "problem" orientation. A control orientation during an interview means that you keep complete control over the interviewee. He has no say in what happens. With a problem orientation, you suggest that "we have a problem" rather than "you have a problem."

Some years ago, management of a major airline protested that there was no money for employee salary raises. In fact, they suggested that employees and management faced a common problem: Without drastic action, the company was going bankrupt. Using a "we have a common problem" approach, management was able to focus everyone's attention on their common concerns. They developed a compromise that included temporary salary reductions and a future profit-sharing plan. This helped the company avoid bankruptcy and kept the employees' jobs intact. Had the company attempted to control employees and their union by maintaining that the employees had a problem and had better cut down on their wage demands, the outcome could have been tragically different.

Separate Person from Behavior

In delivering bad news it is important that you separate the person from the behavior. It is possible that when refusing an individual, he will get the impression that the interviewer thinks he is a "bad person." It is better to suggest that "missing on project deadlines is not productive" than to tell an employee that he is a "bad employee."

In the second example, the specific activity is labeled "bad," although the person is not led to believe that he is in fact a bad person. This is an important part of one's counselor role. It does little good to identify a person as bad or to attack him as an individual. What is important is that unproductive behaviors be identified and some standards set for correcting those behaviors.

The interviewee should be shown the "bigger picture" and helped to identify certain behaviors that are counterproductive. It is also important to reduce as much uncertainty as possible. People should be told what to expect and how to behave if they want to be more favorably considered.

Feelings of Urgency

When interviewing, be aware of feelings of urgency. Many interviewers have been trapped by a sense of real or artificial urgency created by the person they are interviewing. When this happens, interviewers lose control of the entire interview.

Be careful not to find yourself stampeded into implying that certain actions will be taken or suggesting that certain concessions might be made. Here again, a middle-ground approach is the most appropriate response. The interviewer should not "give away the store" responding to a sense of urgency or go strictly by the book, ignoring all human consideration and reasons for modifying criteria.

A Superior Attitude

Don't present a superior attitude. Remember that various status symbols, including the size of your desk or the fact that you are sitting behind it, create status barriers that make the interviewer appear superior.

The superiority can also be demonstrated by such body language as leaning back in your chair as far away as possible from the interviewee or having the fingers of both hands touching and pointing up in a "steeple" gesture. Whenever possible, minimize the differences and distance between the interviewer and the interviewee. By reducing the personal distance between people, it is possible to create a greater feeling of warmth and rapport without breaking the normal barriers that should exist between interviewer and interviewee.

Be cautious that your attempt to reduce superiority not be perceived as manipulation. When people perceive manipulation, they frequently become defensive and tend to assume that "you are out to get me." When this happens, the best approach is to back off and possibly reschedule the interview for another day.

Minimize Negatives

Don't give yourself away. When giving bad-news messages to people in an interview situation, it is wise to avoid references to the bad news that will be coming. This is a strategy similar to writing a bad-news letter. As much as possible, try to avoid such statements as, "You are not going to like what I am going to say in a few minutes." These statements needlessly increase anxiety and do very little good.

We often use such statements to prepare ourselves to deliver a bad-news message. This sort of message does not really help the receiver understand or accept the bad news. It is better to hide negative messages by first building your case, explaining reasons in a "you viewpoint." When the time comes for the bad news, make it as specific as possible, while minimizing the causes of defensiveness.

CLOSING THE INTERVIEW

As you close an interview, especially one in which bad news has been discussed, try to close in an upbeat tone. Above all, don't recall the problem or continue to backslap in an attempt to overcome the negative effects of the bad news. It is far better to leave the interviewee feeling that she has had a full hearing than it is to have you suggest, "I really wish we could have helped you." Such statements recall the whole problem.

If you have successfully reduced some of the personal threat while delivering the bad message, such a closing may undo all the good work that you have already done. *Don't make the other person appear stupid* or unworthy. Make it clear throughout the interview that the other person's interests are also your main concern. This can be done by avoiding statements such as "everyone knows that . . ." or "obviously you must have known . . ." or "only a fool would do such and such." These statements unnecessarily antagonize the interviewee and serve no useful purpose except perhaps to relieve some of the pressure from you.

In an interview, try to *avoid rapid shifts in logic.* Don't make leaps from one topic to another without giving the other person some notion of the reason for the transition you are making or at least some idea of where you are going with your questions.

Rapid shifts may be appropriate in a movie, but they have no place in an interview where the objective is to develop rapport and contact between you and someone else.

Avoid negative tones of voice or the "accusatory" sound that we sometimes have in our voices, especially when asking for additional information. If additional information is required, don't give the impression that you need the information because you don't trust the other person or feel his answers are evasive. Rather, explain that the information you now have is insufficient and that you would therefore like to have some additional information in a certain area.

Finally, and most important in any interview, be yourself. Interviewing is not a talent that most people have naturally. Rather, it involves learned skills and learned behaviors. The way you behave with a member or employee is not necessarily the way you would behave with friends or family.

However, your success as an interviewer, measured in terms of personal satisfaction and organizational success, is directly related to your communication ability. As organizations become more complex, we increasingly hear the complaint that they are impersonal, that "they don't think of me as an individual." There is much we can do to overcome this perception by maintaining a personable, informal, and skilled manner in interviewing and in other public or private transactions.

Keep your mind on the objectives of your interview and listen for the subtle messages the interviewer may be sending. You'll find your effectiveness and personal satisfaction as an interviewer greatly enhanced.

5

The Employment Interview: Do's and Don'ts

In the last chapter we discussed many of the problems and situations that arise in any interview. In this chapter, we will look more closely at the employment interview.

An employment interview is conducted for several reasons, the main reason being to learn more about the people under consideration for a particular job. In some organizations, the employment interview for hourly paid, nonmanagement positions is simple. The sole responsibility of the interviewer is to verify the answers the prospective employee has given on the company application form. Even in such a simple interview, there should be an opportunity for the prospective employee to ask questions, clarify company policies, and generally get acquainted with the organization. In other organizations, every candidate for every job being filled is given an in-depth interview. Management is interested in going beyond the answers to the questions in the application. Questions asked of the interviewee deal with attitudes toward work, co-workers, unions, working conditions, customers, clients, patients, and products. As management's attention has been focused increasingly on productivity, there is more productivity-oriented questioning done in interviews. Most organizations subject their prospective management people to in-depth interviews, often with multiple interviewers. In short, careful, meaningful interviewing is on the rise.

Unfortunately, the need for more careful interviewing does not result in better interviewing. Too often, managers use their own experience when they were hired as the guide for conducting employment interviews. There is nothing wrong with this kind of preparation, if the interviewing was done recently, and by competent interviewers. If the person doing the interviewing is relying on personal experience from several years ago, it is likely that she is using outmoded and possibly illegal interview questions and techniques. And if the person or persons who interviewed those now doing the interviewing were poor models, the result today may be poor interviewing.

THE LAW IS CLEAR, ISN'T IT?

There are many areas of employment interviewing that are covered in the various regulations and pronouncements of the Equal Employment Opportunity Commission (EEOC), or in the regulations of various state employment agencies. Some of these regulations are specific: for example, the prohibition of questions related to sex, race, national origin, religious preference, and age. The catch is that questions in any of these areas *may* be perfectly proper and legal, if they meet the test of being "bona fide occupational qualifications" (BFOQ). Other regulations deal with the fuzzier aspects of these sensitive topics. For example, an employment interviewer may not ask a prospective female employee if she has suitable arrangements for child care during working hours.

If these examples are not enough, consider the effects of various court and administrative law rulings on the employment interiew process. As cases are brought before judicial bodies at the local, state, or federal level, new law is put into effect. Each case either upholds a previous interpretation of a law, rule, or regulation, or it establishes new precedent. In some cases, the precedents are binding on all employment interviews in all companies. In other cases, the decisions by the courts apply only to the specific case tried and decided.

Then there is the matter of new administrative rulings. Government agencies at various levels are constantly monitoring practices in employment and issuing new or revised regulations to take care of new or previously unanticipated situations. Thus what may have been marginally legal one day may be prohibited or illegal the next.

Finally, there are new laws being passed constantly. Some of these new laws amend old laws; others establish controls in previously uncontrolled areas of employment. Some of these laws or revisions favor the companies doing the hiring. In other cases, they favor the person being interviewed and considered for employment.

Combine all of these considerations with the changing nature of the work force and the complexity of today's work environment, and it is impossible to say precisely what can and cannot be done or asked during employment interviews.

With these considerations in mind, let's look at some of the general limitations and boundaries that affect an employment selection interview—both the "do's" and the longer list of "don'ts."

Pre- and Postemployment Questions

To avoid opportunities for discrimination, or to avoid the appearance of an intention to discriminate, the law prohibits employers from asking certain questions or delving into certain areas. However, for many good reasons, employers may need to know certain sensitive information about their employees in order to comply with other laws or to provide for the employee's safety and security.

For example, an employer is not allowed to ask a prospective employee's race. Yet some affirmitive action commitments or government contracts require employers to report on the racial composition of their work force. How does this apparent dilemma get resolved?

The answer is to distinguish between preemployment and post-employment questions.

The law is most restrictive in the preemployment question area. No information that in any way deals with race, sex, age, religious preferences, or national origin can be asked. After a person is hired, however, an employer may ask for certain sensitive data about employees *as long as such information is maintained in files that are not used for later promotion consideration.*

In short, you can ask an employee for a lot of information you cannot ask her as an interviewee.

In the following sections of this chapter, we will look at several examples of pre- and postemployment questioning, indicating the kinds of information that can be asked before and after a hire decision has been made.

WHAT CANNOT BE ASKED

The basic law covering selection interviewing is the 1964 Civil Rights Act, Title VII, and amendments in 1968 and 1972. Key sections of this law state the following:

Sec. 703
(a) It shall be unlawful employment practice for an employer—
(1) to fail or refuse to hire or to discharge any individual, or otherwise to discriminate against any individual with respect to his compensation, terms, conditions, or privileges of employment, because of such individual's race, color, religion, sex, or national origin; or

(2) to limit, segregate, or classify his employees or applicants for employment in any way which would deprive or tend to deprive any individual of employment opportunities or otherwise adversely affect his status as an employee, because of such individual's race, color, religion, sex, or national origin.

(b) It shall be an unlawful employment practice for an employment agency to fail or refuse to refer for employment, or otherwise to discriminate against, any individual because of his race, color, religion, sex, or national origin, or to classify or refer for employment any individual on the basis of his race, color, religion, sex, or national origin.

(c) It shall be an unlawful employment practice for a labor organization—
(1) to exclude or to expel from its membership or otherwise to discriminate against, any individual because of his race, color, religion, sex, or national origin;

(2) to limit, segregate, or classify its membership or applicants for membership or to classify or fail or refuse to refer for employment

any individual in any way which would deprive or tend to deprive any individual of employment opportunities, or would limit such employment opportunities or otherwise adversely affect his status as an employee or as an applicant for employment, because of such individual's race, color, religion, sex, or national origin; or

(3) to cause or attempt to cause an employer to discriminate against an individual in violation of this section.

(d) It shall be an unlawful employment practice for any employer, labor organization, or joint labor-management committee controlling apprenticeship or other training or retraining, including on-the-job training programs to discriminate against any individual because of his race, color, religion, sex, or national origin in admission to, or employment in, any program established to provide apprenticeship or other training.

Sec. 704.
(b) It shall be an unlawful employment practice for an employer, labor organization, employment agency, or joint labor management committee controlling apprenticeship or other training or retraining, including on-the-job training programs to print or cause to be printed or published any notice or advertisement relating to employment by such an employer or membership in or any classification or referral for employment by such a labor organization, or relating to any classification or referral for employment by such an employment agency, or relating to admission to, or employment in, any program established to provide apprenticeship or other training by such a joint labor-management committee indicating any preference, limitation, specification, or discrimination, based on race, color, religion, sex, or national origin.[1]

Interpreting the Civil Rights law, following are some do's and don'ts in selection interviewing.

Creed or Religious Preference.   You cannot ask for a person's religious preference. You cannot ask for the name of the person's priest, rabbi, or minister, and you cannot ask for a religious reference or a personal reference from a member of the clergy. If there is a bona fide reason for considering one's religious preferences and beliefs in the hiring process, such questions may be asked.

Suppose you operate a business that requires employees to work on days kept as a sabbath by certain denominations. In this case, you can *inform* the prospective employee of the working days—or any other working conditions that might cause a moral conflict for an employee. This way, it is up to the individual to decide if such conditions are compatible with his religious preferences. Many employers who have working conditions that conflict with religious practices try to make arrangements so that no employee is unnecessarily put in a conflicting position. However, such arrangements are not required of employers.

After a person has been hired, it may be permissible to ask for the name of a member of the clergy to be notified in case of emergency. In one company, management was permitted to inquire about the religious preferences of their employees because there was a bona fide reason. The company provided free meals to their people and wanted to offer selections that respected the dietary observances of certain faiths and denominations.

Race or Color.   You cannot ask about a person's race, skin color, or racial heritage. You cannot make any notation on a resume, application form, or interview summary that indicates race or color.

Although not related to race, there are some physical appearance characteristics you may be permitted to note. For example, it is all right to note scars, blemishes, tatoos, or other identifying marks. However, such information is not likely to be relevant to the hiring decision; therefore, such questions are better left until postemployment.

Sex.   You cannot make any inquiry related to sex. You cannot advertise or announce that a job is open to men only because it requires heavy lifting. You can specify that the job requires heavy lifting, even if such a specification tends to limit the number of women who qualify.

Sex can be a factor in hiring if it is a bona fide occupational qualification. For example, the job of gynecologist's assistant may be a woman-only job because it relates to the privacy of the doctor's female patients. A men's room attendant would be a similar example.

Failure to have facilities for persons of both sexes is not a bona fide reason for sex discrimination. The courts have held that employers must make a reasonable effort to provide such facilities.

You are not permitted to ask if a woman prefers to be addressed as Mrs., Miss, or Ms.

Marital Status.   You cannot ask if a prospective employee is married, single, widowed, or divorced. You cannot ask for any information about the person's spouse or where she is employed. You cannot ask for number of children, their ages, or about the person's future family plans or about birth control or family planning methods now used or contemplated.

You can inform a prospective employee about a company policy prohibiting employment of two persons married to one another. You can inform the prospect that the job requires frequent relocation, extended travel, or travel on short notice. You may inform prospects about company-sponsored or -supported child-care facilities.

Pregnancy is not a bona fide reason to refuse employment, although it can (and should) be a consideration in temporary work assignments.

Height and Weight.   Questions about height and weight are permissible as long as they relate to bona fide occupational qualifications. For example, persons over a certain weight may not be able to fit in the confined quarters of a commercial airliner and would be unsuited for such jobs as cabin attendant or maintenance inspector. Persons above or below a certain height range may not be able to properly operate equipment that cannot be adjusted for height differences.

Weight or height restrictions must be bona fide, however, to avoid unnecessary racial or ethnic discrimination. For example, high minimum height standards may discriminate against Orientals, whose mean height is generally lower than the mean height of other groups.

Disability.   You are not permitted to ask a prospective employee if he has any disabilities, and you are not permitted to ask if he has been treated for some list of specified diseases. Both inquiries are considered intrusions into the individual's privacy in an area where there is no legitimate occupational connection. You can ask if the individual has any physical, mental, or medical impairments that would interfere with the successful performance of the job for which the individual is applying. You can inform the applicant of unusual, stressful, hazardous, or uncomfortable conditions in the work or workplace that might aggravate certain physical conditions, but the decision to communicate disability information is the employee's.

If the individual is not applying for a specific job, or if there are several openings for which the individual is being considered, it is permissible for the interviewer to ask if there are any jobs or types of positions for which she should not be considered, or if there are any job requirements that the individual cannot perform because of disabilities. This sort of question protects the individual's medical or disability privacy while informing the interviewer of potential job-related problems.

If an applicant does volunteer that there are positions or job requirements that he cannot handle, the interviewer is not permitted to inquire about the specific disability.

Arrest Record.   You cannot ask an applicant if she has ever been arrested. You can ask the applicant if she has ever been convicted of a crime, and if so, what the details of that crime were. Some organizations avoid the arrest question by using the stringent requirements of a bonding company. The applicant is informed that the job for which she is applying requires that the employee be bonded. Then the applicant is informed about the requirements of the bonding company and is asked if there is anything in her background that would prevent her from being bonded. Of course, if the employee says that bonding would not be possible, questioning can only proceed in the area of convictions, not arrests.

Keep in mind that in order to have a bonding requirement as a part of a job specification, there must be a bona fide reason for doing so.

Name.   You mean you can't even ask an applicant his name?

It's not quite that serious. What you cannot ask an applicant is his former name if it has been changed by the courts. Most married women have had their legal names changed by court order at the time they were married, and many men and women have had some changes for a variety of reasons. You cannot ask for a woman's maiden name, nor can you ask a person why her name was changed. You can ask the applicant if she has ever worked for your company under a different name, and you can ask if the applicant has any other legal names, assumed names, or nicknames that are necessary in order to complete a check of her work record.

Address or Duration of Residence.   You cannot ask an applicant for any past foreign addresses. However, with this exception, there are no other restrictions on information on address. You can ask for an applicant's current place of residence, how long he has lived at that address, and how long he has been a resident of a particular city or state. You can ask for former residences if there is a reasonable reason for doing so (such as a person who has lived at a present address for less than two or three years). You cannot ask an applicant if he rents or owns his current residence.

Birthplace.   You cannot ask for an applicant's birthplace, or for the birthplace of the applicant's parents, spouse, children, or other relatives.

Birth Date and Age.   You cannot ask an applicant's age. You cannot require a birth certificate or other birth record (such as a certificate of naturalized citizenship or of baptism). In the case of minors, you can ask if the individual, after accepting employment, will be able to submit some (unspecified) proof that he is of legal age to perform the job. In the area of discrimination on the basis of age, the Age Discrimination in Employment Act of 1967 prohibits age discrimination against those aged sixty to sixty-five. It does permit discrimination against those below the minimum legal age for certain jobs or occupations as set by state statute. Current court and congressional actions with respect to the upper limits of age discrimination suggest that there are few if any reasonable grounds for discriminating against older employees (those older than sixty-five). As of this writing, the minimum age mandatory retirement and other age-based discrimination is seventy, and it is likely to be completely eliminated. Thus, all persons over forty will be protected against discrimination in hiring, promotion, and job assignment based on age.

Citizenship.   You cannot ask an applicant about his country of citizenship. You cannot ask if an applicant is a naturalized or native-born citizen (despite the fact the United States Constitution discriminates in favor of natural-born citizens for the positions of president and vice-president). You cannot ask if an applicant's parents, spouse, children, or close relatives are U.S. citizens, and you cannot ask for an applicant's naturalization papers. You cannot ask the date of a person's naturalization.

You can ask if the applicant is a citizen of the United States. If the applicant is not a U.S. citizen, you can ask if she intends to become a naturalized citizen. Also, it is permissible to ask a noncitizen if she is legally permitted to permanently remain in the United States, and if she intends to permanently remain in this country.

National Origin.   You cannot ask an applicant for the names, addresses, ages, or citizenship status of her relatives. You cannot—even innocently, or because of your own curiosity—ask a person for the derivation or origin of her name. (For example, "Kowalski, that's Polish, isn't it?")You cannot ask for the applicant's "mother tongue."

Languages.   As we noted above, you cannot ask for an applicant's mother tongue, the language the applicant spoke as a child, or the language the applicant speaks at home. You cannot ask how an applicant learned to read, write, or converse in a foreign language. You can ask what languages, if any, the applicant speaks fluently. You can ask about the applicant's proficiency in particular languages, such as reading ability, writing ability, or translation ability.

Relatives.   You cannot ask for the names, addresses, or citizenship status of an applicant's relatives. You cannot ask about the applicant's relatives' national origin. You can ask if the applicant has relatives presently employed by the company, and as noted earlier, you can inform the applicant about company policies concerning the employment of relatives.

Notice in Case of Emergency. You cannot ask an applicant for the name of a relative to be contacted in case of an emergency. You can ask for the name of a person to be contacted in case of emergency. However, because most applicants list relatives as the persons to be notified, most employers find it prudent to ask for such information after the individual has been hired.

Military Experience. There are no restrictions on questions concerning a person's military service unless those questions fall into other areas already discussed. For example, you cannot inquire if an applicant has served in the military forces of a foreign country. However, you can ask about the applicant's service experience in the armed forces of the United States or in state militia organizations. You can ask if the person was honorably discharged, although caution should be exercised in probing into the details of discharges other than honorable.

Organizational Memberships. You cannot ask an interviewee for a list of all the organizations he belongs to, or for a list of past organizational memberships. You cannot inquire into a person's labor union membership, past or present, and it is not a prudent idea to ask about a person's preferences toward organized labor in general. You can ask about the applicant's membership in specific organizations that may have some relevance to the position the person is applying for. It is also permissible to ask the applicant to list those organizational memberships he feels are relevant to his ability to perform on the job. For example, asking such a general job-related question might elicit the response, "I'm a member of the Board of Directors of the American Society of Engineers, and I've been a member of the organization for twelve years." Such information about the applicant indicates professional commitment and peer acceptance. It may also indicate to the interviewer that the applicant has already made some time commitments that could possibly interfere with work activities. Such inquiries are quite permissible.

Banks and Credit. You cannot ask an applicant for a specific bank reference, and you cannot ask about his credit rating. However, there are no general prohibitions currently in force that prohibit a prospective employer from using a standard credit rating check as a part of a review of a person's background prior to employment. Such a practice is controversial and will doubtless be a focus of legislation and court action in the near future.

Education.   You cannot ask about a person's religious training, and you cannot ask for details on race, ethnic origin, sex, or nationality that might arise in connection with a person's educational background. For example, you cannot inquire about a person's religious affiliations based on his attendance at Southern Methodist University, Temple Beth Shalom High School, Central Catholic High School, or similar institutions. This is the only restriction on questions about a person's educational background and preparation.

Work Experience.   As with education, there are no areas of a person's work experience that are covered by prohibitions, unless those questions lap over into areas otherwise covered. As we will discuss below, education and work experience are two areas where most of the preemployment interview should be focused.

Testing.   Testing is not an interviewing issue, but it does fall into the area of employment practices. Because of the enactment of the civil rights laws and amendments and the actions of the EEOC, the use of psychological and personality testing in employment has largely been discontinued. What testing is done as a part of the hiring process is in the areas of skill and proficiency tests, mechanical aptitude and clerical tests, or tests dealing with a specific body of knowledge required for certain jobs. Apart from the scientific issues of the validity and reliability of psychological tests, there is a concern that certain such tests have built-in cultural or ethnic biases that can, when interpreted and used as the basis for hiring, result in discrimination. Although most of the objection to such testing has focused on racial discrimination, interpretive statements in the 1964 Civil Rights Act suggest that the Congress was also concerned about the biases in testing that result in discrimination toward older employees. Specifically, the 1964 law refers to the "test-sophistication" of younger people,[2] and suggests that this is another reason for limited and strictly controlled use of psychological testing.

   In short, employers are wise to avoid using psychological or general intelligence tests as part of the employment process unless the tests have been subjected to considerate validation and reliabiliity surveying, and unless the tests being used have been approved by the EEOC.

Photographs.   Interviewers are not permitted to ask an applicant for a photograph, and they are not permitted to attach any photograph of the applicant to the application form or the applicant's file. Many interviewers who receive unsolicited résumes from prospective employees have adopted a policy of removing photographs from the resumes before filing them. There is a feeling that having photographs of prospective candidates in preemployment files may be considered evidence of intent to discriminate, even if the photographs were voluntarily provided by the applicant.

You can inform the candidate that after he is hired, photographs will be taken for identification purpose. Photographs can be taken of any employees for any bona fide reason.

The Application Form Itself.   During most employment interviews, the person doing the interviewing has a copy of an application form, completed by the applicant, available for reference. This form, or a résumé prepared by the applicant, serves as the basis for the interview questions and is then used for evaluation of the candidates after the interviews are completed. When interviewers are talking with several candidates for a particular job, there is often some difficulty in remembering which candidate was which. As we noted above, photographs are not permitted in a candidate's employment file. Therefore, there is a temptation to put some sort of note either in the candidate's file or on the application form to identify the individual. These notes, which may be solely for the convenience of the interviewer and used only to differentiate candidates (with no intention to discriminate) may seem harmless. For example: "black female, 30ish," "50ish male, tall" "Oriental, nice smile."

All such notes, or any coding system that represents the same information, is taboo, either on the application forms or in the candidate's file. Having such information, even when recorded in the interviewer's personal code, may be considered by the EEOC or the courts to be prima facie evidence of intent to discriminate. Don't do it.

WHAT CAN BE ASKED

By the time we finish discussing what we cannot ask during an employment interview, it is logical to ask what questions we can ask of prospects that will give us the information we need to make our decision. There are all kinds of questions we can and should ask prospective employees. None of these questions violate any individual's rights, yet they can provide us with useful and relevant information. Let's look at some of the kinds of questions we can ask.

Questions for Answers
Not Just Responses

Ask questions that force the interviewee to give you an answer, instead of a yes/no response. This means avoiding such questions as the following:

- Do you like your present job?
- Are you satisfied with your career progress?
- Do you find other people helpful?
- Do you set goals for yourself?
- Do you get rattled when things go wrong?
- Do you make good decisions?
- Can you handle people problems?
- Do you have to be checked on to get things done on the job?

Unless you are prepared to wait for a detailed answer, or unless you have a follow-up question ready, all you'll get from these questions is a yes or a no.

Let's use our eight examples, turning them into meaningful questions.

- What are your favorite challenges on your present job?
- What kinds of career progress have you been making so far?
- What do your co-workers do for you that you find helpful?
- What are your goals?
- What do you do when things go wrong?
- How do you make decisions? How do you evaluate the decisions you make?
- What in your view is the ideal way to handle people problems?
- What kind of supervisory style brings out the best in your job performance?

All of these questions ask for general information—which can be very useful in forming a complete image of the prospective employee in the interviewer's mind.

Questions
About Work Experience

One of the best indicators of future performance on the job is an individual's past work experience. Work experience also offers the broadest and largest range of questioning opportunities. Following are some typical work experience questions:

- Where have you worked before?
- Tell me about your last job (or about some particular job listed on the application form).
- Why did you leave XYZ Co.?
- Why did you go to work for ABC Co.?
- Can you describe a typical day on your present job?
- What kinds of decisions do you feel most qualified to make? Least qualified to make?
- If you could find or design it, what would your perfect or ideal job be?
- What parts of your present job give you the most trouble?
- What kinds of employees do you least like to work with?
- How successful do you feel you've been in your career?
- What kind of work record did you compile at your last firm? What do you think your boss would say about your work performance, attendance record, etc.?

We've examined some general questions in the areas of work history. Let's now look at some work history that deal with specifics.

Level and complexity of the applicant's work
- What kinds of things did you do in your job with Daylex?
- Can you describe a typical day on the job?
- What kinds of activities took up most of your time on your job? Of the people you worked for or with, which ones seemed to place the greatest number of time demands on you?
- What kinds of decisions did you make on your job?

Extent of job responsibilities
- Where did you fit on the Daylex organization chart?
- What were your boss's major job responsibilities?
- How did you and your boss share responsibilities and assignments?
- What kind of staff did you personally control?
- How much money could you spend without someone else's approval?
- What were some of the major decisions you made without consulting your boss?

Motivation

- Why did you go to work with Daylex in the first place?
- Why are you leaving Daylex?
- What kinds of other changes in your life are accompanying your job change?
- Why did you stay with Daylex for as long as you have?
- Could you describe what you consider to be the perfect job for you and how close your last job came to being a perfect job?

Attitudes

- What do you find most satisfying in a job?
- What are your feelings—in general—about Daylex?
- What are your present feelings about your present boss?
- What kind of climate do you think there is at Daylex? How could it be improved?
- What aspects of your last job provided you with the most challenge?
- What aspects provided the least challenge?
- How do you feel about the progress you've made in your career up to this point?

Job Performance

- How much did your earnings increase during your time at Daylex? What effect did your work performance have on those increases?
- What was your single most important accomplishment for the company while you were with Daylex? What was your most significant *personal* accomplishment during that time?
- How did your boss feel about the job you did?
- What kinds of things do you think your boss will mention in her recommendation for you?
- What were some of the tough problems you had to handle? How did your handling of those problems come out?

Of course, with all of these questions and others like them, every effort should be made to avoid giving the applicant the impression he is being "grilled" or subjected to the third degree. On the other hand, these questions, and the follow-up questions that they will generate, can give you some useful insights into a person's background and work history that mere facts cannot provide.

Questions About Education

As we have noted, work history and education are two areas where there is an almost unlimited range of questions open to an interviewer. Every effort should be made to use these questions to learn more about the interviewee. Following are some sample questions that one can ask in the area of educational background and training history.

Areas of study

- What were your major courses of study while you were in school?
- What were your minor subject areas in school? Why did you choose them?
- What elective courses did you take in school?
- What kinds of formal continuing education or professional development training have you taken since going to work for Daylex (or since leaving secondary school or college)?
- Describe how and what you did as a student.

Academic Performance

- What kind of grades did you get in school? What were your grades in your major courses?
- How well did you do in school?
- What were your best subjects? What were your worst subjects?
- What courses did you get the most out of? What courses did the least for you?
- Do your grades give you a fair and accurate picture of what you learned in school?
- Apart from any formal class ranking number, where do you think you stood (stand) with regard to the quality and performance of your classmates?

Attitudes

- Why did you go to this (that, these, those) school(s)?
- Were your expectations of what you'd get from your schooling met, or did you find yourself disappointed with your education?
- What did you like best about State U?
- Do you feel your education was worthwhile?
- What courses did you take that you feel will best equip you for success with this company?
- If you had the same decision to make again, would you choose to go to the same school? Would you take the same major, courses, teachers?

Motivation

- Why did you choose that particular major?
- Why did you change schools in the middle of your degree program?
- Do you plan to complete your education while working? How much more education do you feel you will need before you feel educated?
- If you had to choose only one course to take in a formal educational setting, which course would it be?

Student Activities

- While you were a student, what organizations did you join? How active were you in those organizations? What offices did you hold in those organizations?
- Did you ever join an organization and then decide to drop your membership? Why?
- Why did you choose to join the _____ organization? What did your membership in that organization do for you?
- Do you plan to maintain your contact with your student organizations now that you're in the "adult" world?
- What was one accomplishment outside of the classroom that you feel particularly good about?
- How did you pay for your education?
- Do you feel that grades are the best basis for judging a prospective employee, or should his extracurricular activities also be considered?
- Which activities are more important while a person is in school— social, professional, athletic, general interest?
- If you had a choice between a person with high grades and no extra-curricular activities and a person with average grades and a record of involvement in extracurricular activities, which would you hire? Why?

Work history and education questions should give you an insight into the applicant's motivation, background, and appropriateness for a particular job. Care should be taken to follow up all questions while looking for those areas where additional information might yield useful additional insights. Often, simply asking why is enough to bring out the reality of hidden answers and comments.

TYPES OF QUESTIONS

There are three broad kinds of questions that an interviewer can and should ask. They are the motive question, the personal qualification question, and the "tough" question. Let's look at each of them briefly.

The Motive Question

A motive question is any question that seeks to determine, directly or indirectly, if the interviewee will really enjoy doing the job for which she is being considered, or if the job will merely be "a job." Later in this book, we will discuss some approaches to firing people who do not perform as they should. A major reason for having to do such firing is a failure to motivate the individual, or an individual's failure to enjoy the job she is doing. Thus the importance of asking questions that go to the heart of the motivation issue.

In asking motive questions, the interviewer is going into a person's likes, dislikes, ambitions, and desires. They include such questions as the following:

- Do you prefer working for a large or small company?
- What do you want to be doing in ten years? Realistically, what will you be doing in ten years?
- What constitutes an "ideal" job for you? Why?
- What are your major strengths and weaknesses?
- Are you a self-starter, or do you like to be closely supervised?
- Are you a person who likes to work alone, or are you a "team player"?
- If you did not have to work for a living, what would you be doing?

In asking motive questions, it is important that the interviewer not "telegraph" to the applicant the acceptable answers. Good listeners can often learn from the way a question is worded what answer the interviewer would like to have. When an interviewer gets this phony feedback, there is a danger that an incorrect or inaccurate evaluation will result. Therefore, it is useful to ask motivation questions early in an interview, before the person being interviewed knows too much about either the job or the person doing the interviewing.

When listening for the answers to motive questions, consider more than just the answer. Listen for the confidence in the interviewee's voice. Watch for signs of discomfort or hesitation. How long did he pause before answering? Pausing too long may indicate unsureness or shallowness (not having thought through the item earlier). Pausing too little, or not at all, may indicate a prepared or even memorized answer, which may not be an accurate indication of how the interviewee truly feels. How long is "too long"? There is the problem. The right length of the pause between the end of a question and the beginning of an answer is highly subjective.

While thinking about motive questions, notice how enthusiastic the interviewee is about the job and the company. Often, the amount of preparation the candidate did on the company (and even the interviewer) is an indication of his motivation. If the interviewee apparently knows little about the company, it may be a good indication of a lack of motivation. On the other hand, if the candidate knows something about the company, its product, customers, and competitors, there is strong evidence of advance study and preparation. Some other ways to probe a candidate's motivation is to note the number, kinds, and quality of questions the interviewee asks. Did the questions range over a number of concerns, or did they focus primarily on benefits, compensation, hours, and work locations?

As we mentioned above, many interviewees are skilled at being interviewed. They will have prepared answers to some of the more difficult questions, and they will be able to give back to the interviewer the kinds of answers they think are appropriate, not necessarily accurate or honest answers. Care should be taken that too much emphasis or weight is not given to motive question answers when making the hiring decision. If you are really interested in delving into a person's motivations and you consider such factors to be highly important in making your decision, you might be wise to retain a psychologist or other professional who is trained to listen and to evaluate psychological responses.

The Personal Qualifications Questions

The personal qualifications question is another type of question that interviewers can (and should) ask as a part of the employment interviewing process. In general, a personal qualifications question is an attempt to probe a prospective employee in terms of his attributes, traits, and other relevant qualifications. Each time we interview someone for a position, we should have firmly fixed in our mind a list of qualifications an ideal employee would have. These qualifications should relate to the person as a person and as an employee rather than to any racial, ethnic, sexual, age, or other characteristics. This list of qualifications would include some indication of whether the particular characteristic is something you would like to have in an employee, or if it is something you absolutely must have.

The list of personal qualifications is virtually limitless. There are a number of directions such questions can go in. For example:

- What kind of employee (manager, accountant) are you?
- How do you perform under pressure?
- Are you a self-starter? Can you work without direct supervision?
- How long will it be before you are a contributing part of our organization?

All of these questions require considerable thought and self-analysis on the part of the interviewee. They give the interviewee a chance to give some flattering and self-serving answers. This may tempt the interviewee to overstate or exaggerate and to get caught doing so. Analyzing answers to personal qualifications questions usually requires some reading between the lines. One way to do this is to ask the interviewee for evidence to support his answers. Use caution. Don't get caught allowing the interviewee to get away with casual or unsupported statements.

On the other hand, confine personal qualifications to important personal qualities. The number of such questions will vary, depending on how well (and thoroughly) the candidate's past record of work and education has been explored. In any case, a selection interview should only include a few personal qualifications questions.

The Tough Questions

Every interview should include a few "tough questions"—questions an interviewer would rather not be forced to answer. When hiring, a major goal is to identify—and to avoid—persons with problems that would adversely affect their job performance.

The best tough questions relate to a person's reasons for leaving present or past jobs. Other good areas for exploration are

- A job-hopping record.
- Periods of unemployment.
- Inconsistencies in other answers.
- Comments with racial, sexist, or ethnic overtones.

Some tough questions focus on these areas. Others require the candidate to identify their own weaknesses. Ask about problems the person has had with supervisors, co-workers, and others, and then discuss what efforts (if any) were made to deal with the problem.

SUMMARY
OF THE INTERVIEW "DO'S"

Following are some of the areas where selection interview questions should go:

1. Questions for more detailed information on items on application forms or resumes.
2. Reasons for leaving former jobs.
3. Speculation about what kinds of references a candidate will receive.
4. Profiles of past job activities and responsibilities.
5. Likes and dislikes the applicant has about her past jobs.
6. The applicant's preferences and desires in the job sought—this

should include preferred hours, wages, assignments, duties, co-workers, etc.

7. Self-evaluation—what the applicant considers his strengths and weaknesses both for the immediate position and for future positions in the company.

8. Any additional information on any subject that the applicant feels is relevant. This is important. The applicant should be permitted an open-ended question to bring up matters not touched on by other questioning. Listening to these volunteered answers can also result in information valuable for making the hire/don't hire decision.

CONCLUSION

Use caution in questioning job applicants. The old rule of thumb—"I won't ask any question I wouldn't want to answer myself"—isn't valid anymore. Too often, illegal, discriminatory, or distasteful questions arise from ignorance rather than from any malice or design. However, the impact on the interviewee (and on the outcome of the interview) is just as devastating. Focus questions on those areas where it is possible to reap useful information. Doing so, there is no need to fear the "don'ts" in interviewing.

6
The Art of
Checking References

You pick up the telephone and dial a number.[1] On the other end of the line is someone you don't know. Yet you are going to ask him some questions about a third party—a former member of his staff— and you expect him to answer these questions.

All of a sudden you wonder: Will he tell me what I need to know, or will he simply say what he thinks I want to hear? A legitimate question, but two better questions yet would be: Why am I making this call? What's a reference really worth?

One school of thought has it that references aren't worth the time expended on them. As one friend of mine, an executive with a sizable company, once put it, "Look, the whole reference bit reminds me of a stage duel. The weapons are sheathed, it makes a good show, and nobody gets killed in the end." But everybody wins. That is, the caller feels virtuous about having made the call—never mind that he got no substantive information—and the reference-giver feels equally virtuous, for hasn't he given Ed, who was never the model employee, a leg up—somewhere else?

That sort of telephone charade is carried out every day a thousand times, and only AT&T is the real winner. Why bother?

"Whoever does the calling," says one top personal director, "feels that he has done his duty."

Meaning, of course, that if his decision to hire the person he has called about is later challenged by higher authority, he can defend himself with the magic words, "But I checked his references." Which is the truth, but not the whole truth.

Much reference calling is perfunctory. The kind of questions asked can yield little information regarding Ed and Ed's capabilities. The caller opens the conversation by asking, "What kind of man is Ed?" and allows Ed's former boss, who is glad to be rid of Ed but anxious not to see him unemployed, to reply vaguely that "Ed is a fine fellow."

Which may, indeed, be the case. That Ed is also lackadaisical and unimaginative is another matter—one that his former boss feels no compulsion to bring up. "After all," he says to himself, "I am telling the truth." Yes—but not the whole truth. But then he has not been asked to, has he?

Many bosses are reluctant to volunteer information which, though not necessarily detrimental, might prevent the Eds of this world from getting another job, whether they were fired or they left by mutual consent. Some humane bosses—are you one of them?—breathe a sigh of relief when the caller limits himself to vague questions that can be answered vaguely.

If you are going to check references, make the calls count.

Before you pick up that phone, ask yourself the following questions: What do I want and need to know about the person I am about to hire? What do I want him to accomplish, and what kind of information will tell me if he is the one to do the job?

Then fashion your questions in such a way that the answers will give you the information you need.

You are about to hire Jim. You have talked to him more than once and at some length and depth about the marketing director's job. Jim has the imagination and drive needed to sell a new product. But—is he a talker or a doer?

Jim has told you that he has informed his current boss that he is looking for another job "to spread my professional wings a little." So you can call the boss.

Knowing what you have in mind—the selling of a new product, the need for the idea that may put it across—you ask, "While Jim has been with you, has your firm put a new product or service on the market? What was Jim's contribution to its success?" Such questions will yield concrete examples of what Jim did and how he did it.

Then you say, "You must be sorry to see him leave." If true, the boss will explain that he cannot afford to keep Jim—perhaps because his operation is smaller than yours—or that he does not feel he can stand in Jim's way.

You have heard what you needed to hear, haven't you? Not quite. Lead into it gently.

"You know," you might say, "Jim is truly sorry to leave you. Given different circumstances, he might have stayed with you for a long time."

The reply you're looking for is, "If we ever grow to the point that we can afford to get him back, I may pirate him from you." Said with a chuckle, but you know that it is meant. That's the best reference of all.

Serious reference-checking is an art and a battle of wits. Some people you call try to deflect questions or give answers to questions not asked, hoping to persuade you that Ed is God's gift to business. It pays to listen.

A friendly, booming voice will tell you that an advertising agency employee is a fabulous writer and a great idea man who knows every radio-TV personality in town.

That's probably true. What the voice neglects to say is that the employee rarely produces copy, that his ideas would put you out of business, and that the radio-TV personalities know him, too. And avoid him.

Note that the voice seized the initiative after your opening sentence and is holding onto it. Before you can think twice, the voice will end it all with a cheery "glad to have been of help." Your ear aches and your brain spins. Yet you have been told nothing.

Some bosses will appear reticent when questioned about job seekers. Charles W. North, Jr., the sophisticated director of personnel of the American Bankers Association, says, "You really don't know when they are telling you the truth. And what complicates it even more, many supervisors are little skilled in giving references. That causes the caller to wonder why they are not more forthcoming."

Such calls can make Ed the victim if you equate reticence with disapproval. Again, the burden is on you. The right questions may loosen up the other party, and what he finally manages to say may make you want to hire Ed. Silence, too, has meaning. I recently called a contact of mine who is well acquainted with a man I was thinking of introducing to a client. My contact is a good evaluator of people.

"Do you think," I said, "that X can successfully do such and such?" (naming a specific area in which my client needed help).

My contact hesitated for a moment. Then he said, "Look, let me put it to you this way . . . "

The hesitation plus the opening phrasing of the answer were enough. "Thanks," I said. "You have told me what I need to know."

A negative reference may mean everything—or nothing. A friend of mine wanted to hire a first-rate engineer and believed he had found one in Walter. Walter had worked for good companies, talked knowledgeably about the job when my friend interviewed him, and was intelligent and thoughtful. Yet when my friend called a former supervisor, the supervisor could not say enough about Walt—all of it bad.

My friend was puzzled and intrigued. How could the derogatory remarks be true, since the engineer had worked for that firm for some time? He decided to call the organization's top executive.

"Hire Walter, by all means," said the executive. "He is first-rate. I was sorry to hear that he was leaving. But I can understand why. His immediate boss hated his guts."

Some references want to protect themselves. The following is what I found in the case of a top executive of a large company whom I called about a former key staffer. "He's all right," the executive said, trying to get off the hook—and off the phone.

"You mean," I persisted, "that he did not do an outstanding job?"

The executive took a deep breath. "That sums it up. Off the record, by the way." What he meant was: I hired him, but I want no one to know that he was just average. The executive laughed, but it was not a cheerful sound. "It took me five years to bite the bullet and suggest that he start looking."

So you see, longevity is not always a sure sign of a winner.

"Some companies," says Philip J. McGovern, a branch manager for Career Blazers Personnel Services, a national employment agency, "make it a policy to divulge only basic facts—length of employment, last salary, that sort of thing. Of course, you can get around that policy if the person you intend to hire has given his immediate supervisor as a reference. The supervisor will probably answer your questions."

Sometimes the person you call will say, "If you write me a letter, I'll answer your questions."

Sounds good? But wait. If the letter asks innocuous questions, it serves no purpose; if it raises sensitive questions, it may spell trouble, should the contents be revealed to the person in question. So think before writing—and possibly discuss it with your attorney.

Let's say you want to hire a man or woman for a key spot and a key reference is acting supercautious. Invite the reference to lunch. Size him up—and then talk turkey. If the other party is out of town, lunch may be impossible, but you might ask whether you could call him at home. If you are refused, find another source of information.

"Rarely," says the personnel director of a large national trade association, "would I call another personnel department to check out someone. You seldom get negative facts from personnel people, and they don't know anything about the person's day-to-day activities."

Calling a personnel department for a reference is all right if the person you are calling about is on the support staff and all you want is to verify employment data.

To get in-depth information about an executive or professional, you have to talk to her superior. The supervisor alone can fill you in on important details you need to know.

"Besides," says a pro in the personnel field, "what counts is that the caller and the called speak the same language, even if they don't know each other personally." For example, if you are a general counsel and the person you call is your opposite number at another company, you can ask questions that outsiders would not think of or consider important, and you can get informative answers.

When you want a professional assessment, a definite "nonsource" is the friend or personal reference. Let him tell you how long he has known John and how punctual and reliable John is in personal contact, but avoid direct sensitive questions, such as on drinking habits.

The answers are rarely reliable, anyway. If John loves the bottle, some former boss may—or may not—tell you. Taking John to lunch may tell you what you need to know.

The ideal reference may be someone not mentioned by—or

even known to—the candidate: a professional acquaintance you have known for years and whose judgment has proven good in the past. He may have been Ed's former boss, or perhaps he has heard about Ed from Ed's former boss, a longtime friend of his. Call him—or, better yet, take him to breakfast. You can ask him sensitive questions ("Is he a chaser, a drunk, a man about town?"), and he will provide negative along with positive facts.

But the buddy system is not infallible. An acquaintance who heads a large organization was ready to make an offer. The candidate's work background seemed above reproach; he had done a fine job for his former employer. What's more, many people in the industry thought highly of him. An ideal candidate.

Yet the executive suddenly decided not to make the offer. Why? Accidentally, some information of a personal nature had come to him, which he had to credit, but which the references could not have known about.

Reference-checking is not foolproof, and references are not infallible. Let your own good judgment be your guide.

That's what one of my clients did, with spectacular success. Told by a reference that the candidate in question "does not seem motivated," he smiled and asked, "Whose fault?" My client promptly hired the candidate, with excellent results for both.

It's one thing to check references, another to use that process as a crutch—or substitute it for your own decision making.

FACING PROBLEMS

7
Understanding Problem Behavior

"He's a *problem employee.*"
"Why do you suppose that is?"
"He's got a lousy *attitude!*"
"Oh! Well, what should he do about it?"
"Simple. *Shape up!*"

This simple dialogue, repeated thousands of times daily, goes straight to the heart of one of the manager's most perplexing and challenging responsibilities—handling the problem employee. It also says a lot about what's wrong with the way many managers handle that employee.

When managers consider the difficulties they face with a problem employee, they often tend to do so in an isolated, "this time only" way. The assumption is that the problem behavior is simply an unproductive or disruptive act that must be punished, or a pattern that must be changed. Problem behavior clearly is a single act or pattern of acts, but it must be viewed in a much larger setting. The individual who engages in "problem" behavior cannot be handled as an individual. He or she is also part of a larger social system, one that must be considered when developing a strategy for combating problem behavior.

If we look at the history of technological inventions, we find a curious and revealing pattern. A great many of the inventions designed to solve specific problems ended up creating more problems than they solved. For example, nuclear power generation is a solution to growing energy needs, yet its invention created massive problems of waste disposal, radiation contamination, and environmental pollution. The automobile, designed to solve the problem of moving people efficiently from one place to another, created (or helped create) such problems as urban sprawl, air pollution, energy depletion, and the "paving" of America. This is not to suggest that these and other inventions are bad, or that they should not have been invented. Rather, it points out the importance of taking a wider or "system" view then trying to solve any problem. Fragmented, piecemeal solutions to technical or human problems are rarely as effective or long lasting as system-wide solutions. It is not enough that automotive engineers try to solve problems of energy depletion with more efficient cars. The "system" of transportation and the philosophies that underlie the system must be treated as a single complex process. In the same way, the individual problem employee or the individual employee problem must be tackled by treating the entire system, of which the employee and the problem are part.

PROBLEM BEHAVIOR
AS A PROCESS

To begin looking at problem behavior as a system, let us develop a model of such behavior. (Figure 4). Each of the components of this model is important, and each contributes to or affects the others. Let's take a closer look at each of the components in the figure.

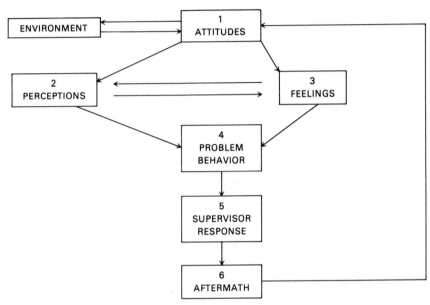

FIGURE 4.

The Environment Dimension

While we are looking at a model of a continuing system of behavior, let's begin our discussion with the environmental part of the process.

As we use the term here, "environment" refers to all the conditions, pressures, attitudes, and influences that surround an individual. The environment is the initial cause of problem behavior, although as we'll discuss shortly, it is not the sole cause.

In the largest sense, environment includes the social, political, economic, religious, and cultural setting in which an individual is raised and presently lives.

If an individual is raised in an environment where drug use is condoned or encouraged, it is likely that the individual will experiment with (and possible abuse) drugs. If the people in one's environment express a lackadaisical attitude toward punctuality, or toward conscientious and productive behavior, the individual is apt to behave in the same way. The environment in effect sets up an individual's potential pattern of behavior through conditioning.

There are other factors in an individual's environment that contribute ultimately to problem behavior. Current social, economic, or family pressures may force an individual to change previous patterns of behavior. For example, severe family pressures may result in increased drinking or drug use. Inflation and economic pressures may force an employee to take a part-time job, resulting in absenteeism, tardiness, and poor performance on her full-time job. Thus, environment has two effects on an individual's behavior. Over a period of time, it influences a person's life-controlling attitudes, and it creates immediate pressures. Of the two, the effect of environment on an individual attitude is perhaps the most important.

In the dialogue at the beginning of the chapter, the problem employee's "problem" was diagnosed as a "bad attitude." Although such a diagnosis is much too simple, it does at least suggest a place to begin looking at an individual's problem behavior.

The Attitude Dimension

Our attitudes, values, and personality are developed from contact with our environment. They develop during our early years as a result of various forces in the environment. During these formative years, attitudes and values will change. However, once our attitudes are fixed or "locked in," it is unlikely that they will change much more than superficially.

According to some experts,[1] we go through "value programming" during our formative years. Like a sponge, we develop values by observing and participating in various processes and activities. During the first five years of life, we are in the "imprinting" stage. Babies listen and respond to everything around them. They may not appear to be paying much attention to their parents, siblings, and others, but they are paying considerable attention. During this stage, family values, religion, and playmate values begin to take effect on the developing individual. The child begins to put together the behaviors he sees, and he connects them with responses. For example, a newborn baby with few attitudes wets his diaper. The response to this behavior is a dry diaper, a pat on the behind, and a little attention. The child begins to associate action (wetting) and response (dry, powder, love), and an attitude takes shape. As this pattern continues, the attitude is reinforced and begins to control the child's behavior. The child may now be wetting the diaper to receive the parent's attention. This pattern of attitude-behavior-response works uninterrupted until one day the behavior is followed by being ignored, or worse, by a slap on the fanny. The attitude that has been controlling the child's behavior has been strengthened, and so the child is apt to assume that this *new* response is just a mistake. Soon, the behavior occurs again, followed by the new response. Still no change in attitude. Now, however, there is a question in the child's mind about why the new responses seems to be replacing the old. Gradually, the child's behavior will change as the child's values adjust to these new inputs of information. This is how values and attitudes are formed during the "imprinting" stage. The impact of the behavior-response cycle and the images and impressions given the child by others results in values being imprinted.

Between the ages of six to twelve, we go through a "modeling" stage. During this period, heroes and role models are very important. It is during this period, some experts suggest, that our values "lock in." From here on, they will be changed only when confronted with some sort of significant emotional event.

In addition to heroes, children in the modeling phase of their development are greatly influenced by their schools, playmates, and by the media that surround them. These media include the influence of books, television, newspapers and films, and also the music they listen to.

In a provocative film,[2] Morris Massey suggests that it is possible to develop considerable insights into anyone's attitudes and values by looking at social, political, economic, and cultural conditions when that person was about ten years old. Massey suggests that what you are today, in terms of your values and attitudes, is a direct result of where you were when you were value programmed. Thus, people who were "modeling" during the 1930s value work, place high importance on security, and generally believe in being self-reliant. People modeled in the 1940s (especially the late 1940s) value affluence and the "good life." Those modeled in the 1950s reflect the rebellion of rock and roll music, and some of their attitudes can be seen in the heroes of the time—James Dean, Elvis Presley, Charles Van Doren. Van Doren in particular is an interesting hero. Praised for his spectacular winnings on a television quiz show, he was later caught in a web of charges of quiz show fixing. To an entire generation of people being modeled, the message may have been "cheating is not bad—getting caught is bad."

People molded in the 1960s tend to reflect the notion of "doing your own thing." Their heroes, such as Joe Namath, were individuals who excelled while flaunting the system.

Watergate, political scandals such as the Korean influence-peddling scheme, and the FBI's "sting" operations against prominent politicians were important aspects of modeling for growing up in the 1970s. The attitudes and values of these young people, the thirty to forty year olds, during the last decade of this century, were shaped and locked in during a time of intense distrust of virtually all social, political, and economic institutions and leaders. Their irreverence, coupled with their disdain of affluence as an end in itself, will begin to make its mark within the decade. It will have an impact on work and productive organizations for many decades to come. Persons who were "modeled" or "value programmed" during the 1960s and 1970s are frequently being referred to as "new generation employees."

The important point about the various attitudes or value systems of various employees is not that some values are right and others wrong. Rather, it is that these value systems often clash. They can lead to radically different perceptions of the "rightness" or "wrongness" of particular actions or attitudes. For example, the person modeled in the 1930s and 1940s places a high value on work and security. Earning a living is a major goal. Since this generation is apt to be typical of many supervisors, there is a potential clash of attitudes when they deal with their employees, who were modeled in the 1950s and 1960s. When the fifty-year-old supervisor finds it necessary to discipline a thirty-year-old worker, the punishment may be a three-day suspension. In the supervisor's mind, three payless days would be a real punishment. But does the younger employee, with different values, see the suspension the same way? The employee may *welcome* the suspension as a sort of vacation. Since his value for economic security is much lower than the supervisor's, the "punishment" isn't likely to change behavior. Instead, a better, more effective punishment is to require the employee to work *overtime*.

This example is not airtight. It suffers the same fate suffered by most generalities; however, it does point out the important role of attitudes and values in the process of employee behavior.

The Perception Dimension

Perception is the process by which we observe, evaluate, and make sense out of our surroundings. Indeed, our ability to communicate is based on our perceptions, and *misperceptions* are a prime cause of communication failures.

Some communication experts like to compare our perceptions with goggles or eyeglasses. It's as though each of us looks at the world and everything in it through a unique, individual pair of goggles. The unique perceptions result in quite different pictures of events, people, or positions. A problem behavior may only be a problem to the supervisor. To the employee doing the behaving, his actions may be normal, justified, and understandable. Co-workers may view the same behavior as a minor annoyance, justified rebellion, or outright blasphemy. Building on the fact that we all see things in a unique way, psychiatrists and psychologists may use shapes made from smears of paint to gauge a patient's mental and emotional state. Think about the shapes we see and the stories we tell when lying on the grass looking up at the clouds. As they change shapes, we form new tales to go with them. The variation in perceptions is also evident in the accounts of eyewitnesses at accidents. Even though many people supposedly "see" the same event, their stories about the event are as varied as it is possible to get. And more to the point about the power of perception is the baseball umpire who declares, "They ain't balls, they ain't strikes! They ain't *nothin'* till I call 'em'."

Although our perceptions affect how we see people, events, and things, a potentially more difficult problem with perceptions is the way they tend to lock us into patterns. Read the following words out loud, quickly, and fill in the word that fits into the blank:

> P-O-L-K is pronounced "poke,"
> F-O-L-K is pronounced, "foke,"
> The white of an egg is the _____.

If you said "yolk" without thinking, try again. The white of an egg is the *white*. Period. Here the perceptual pattern is the sound of the words. Try another:

> If an airplaine crashed *exactly* on the Canadian-American border, where would you bury the survivors?"

Of course, the answer is nowhere—burying survivors is somewhat uncomfortable for them. In this question, the pattern is the relationship between the words *crash*, and *bury*, leading us to confuse "survivors" with "victims."

Read the statement in the triangle in Figure 5. Read it carefully.

FIGURE 5.

JACK
IN THE
THE BOX

How many times did you reread this triangle before you recognized that it *did not* say Jack in the box? The pattern of the familiar words does not allow for a second *the*.

Each of these perception exercises points out the frailty of our perceptions and the difficulty we all have appreciating the viewpoints and perceptions of others. The patterns of our perceptions also tend to lead us to assign arbitrary limits or boundaries to the problems we face. With this thought in mind, consider the nine-dot square (Figure 6).

FIGURE 6.

Here are the instructions: Connect the nine dots with four straight lines, without lifting your pen or pencil from the paper. Take a few minutes to try the puzzle. Reread the instructions, keeping in mind our earlier discussion of boundaries and artificial limits. When (or if) you give up thinking it is impossible to solve this problem, you'll find the answer at the end of this chapter.

As you see, either from your early attempts to solve this problem or from the solution, there's a real temptation to restrict the "solution" to the square area bounded by the outer eight dots. Yet no such instructions were given. Why did you find yourself looking for a solution inside the square? The answer is in the concept of boundary maintenance. We feel more comfortable with limits, boundaries, and territory lines. We respect the boundaries and territories of others. This feeling of looking for and respecting boundaries causes us to attach boundaries even where none exist. We do the same thing to problems and their solutions. We perceive a problem, we try to define it in a way that makes sense to us, and we then respect those problem limits as though they were real. Of course, everyone else in a problem situation is defining her own "problem" and "appropriate solution." The result is often a serious case of missing or distorted perceptions, with each participant in the problem defending to themselves their unique definition and perception of the problem. On an organizational level, this notion of setting boundaries is called tunnel vision. The people in each department or section in an organization come to feel that their work, their objectives, and their problems are more important than anyone else's work, objectives, or problems. Individuals do the same, assuming that their point of view is the only correct point of view, and that all others, even though close, are wrong. When an incident of problem behavior occurs, these strong and differing perceptions will thus cause considerable difficulty for both employee and supervisor.

The Feelings Dimension

Perceptions and feelings are closely related, and they have a great influence on one another. Our feelings about a person depend on what we see—or perceive—about him, and what we perceive is based on our feelings. A mother's loving feelings for a child will color her perceptions of that child's behavior. Thus, in the face of evidence of misbehavior, the feeling of love results in perceptions such as, "No matter what you say, he's a *good boy!*"

On the other hand, our initial feelings about strangers are almost totally based on our perceptions. The way a person looks, is dressed, and the way she engages in small talk are all perceived. Interpretation of these perceptions leads to such statements as, "There's something about him I just don't like" or "I like her—don't know why, but I do."

When we communicate with employees, we do so on two levels. One level is "content." This is the *what* of our message. We also communicate on a "relationship" level, where we express our feelings about one another. These expressions of feelings may be conscious or unconscious. Despite which, they are expressed, and they do have an impact on our behavior.

The Problem Behavior Dimension

All of the environment, attitude and value, perception and feeling dimensions lead ultimately to some sort of behavior. All behavior is determined and affected by these dimensions. Consider the employee who does a good job, behaves in an appropriate manner, and makes valuable contributions leading to cost savings. She does all these things because of her background and the things that go into making up that background. The "good" employee usually is not a concern of managers. Indeed, the productive employee is often taken for granted. Her behavior is simply assumed to be normal, and of little or no concern. The "principle of exception" dictates that managers pay close attention only to those factors that *directly* affect productivity. Keep in mind that while we are looking at the behavior of the problem employee, the productive employee's productive behavior can easily become problem behavior.

When an employee's behavior is a problem, the next logical concern is the reaction of the supervisor or manager. How he or she responds to a problem behavior may not do much about that specific incidence of misbehavior, but it can and will influence future behavior.

The Reaction Dimension

We have learned from studies of individual behavior that it is possible to reinforce an individual's actions by providing the appropriate feedback. When the supervisor's reaction to a behavior episode pleases the employee or satisfies an employee's needs, the employee is being reinforced. As the pattern of behavior-reinforcement continues, the behavior becomes locked in. Thus it is important for the supervisor to carefully consider the reaction to problem behavior.

A hospital administrator faced a problem with one of her department heads. This employee, a man of fifty-three, was constantly coming to work late. He was late nine or ten working days each month. Each time the man was late, the administrator would "visit" with the employee. Did this visit consist of the administrator pointing out to the man that his lateness was a real problem for her and the other supervisors? "Oh, no," she replied, "I wouldn't want him to think I was scolding him." "What did you talk about, then?" we asked. "I asked him about his family, his boat, and we talked about current events, too. That way, he wouldn't think I was putting him down."

This supervisor's reaction to the employee's problem behavior was hardly the sort of reprimand that would cause a change in his behavior. Instead of taking steps to change the behavior, her interest in him may have been satisfying the employee's needs for recognition. The supervisor was reinforcing the problem behavior.

The administrator was finally successful in changing the problem behavior by changing her reaction to each incident. She did so in the following steps:

1. The next time the employee was late, she again visited with him about it, but this time she talked only about the problem behavior. She pointed out the difficulties he was causing by his behavior. She also told him that from here on she would not talk to him again when he was late. She told him she would remind him he was late by giving him a good strong stare, but that was all.
2. The next time the employee was late, she did exactly what she said she would do.

3. On occasional days when the employee arrived for work on time, she would go visit with him and talk about family, fishing, and politics.

The new pattern was now reinforcing positive or productive behavior rather than negative or unproductive behavior.

Suppose a supervisor overreacts to an incident of problem behavior. This can be as potentially damaging as underreacting. In fact, any supervisory reaction will result in an aftermath.

The Aftermath Dimension

It is the aftermath that makes employee problem behavior a process. Technically, the aftermath is the *employee's* reaction to the *supervisor's* reaction to the *employee's* behavior. No matter how the supervisor responds, the aftermath will have an impact on the employee's attitudes and values. For this reason, no problem behavior can be handled as an isolated incident. It is part of a system or pattern of behavior. Everything the employee does is controlled by these attitudes and values, which are themselves being constantly changed and adjusted.

THE LARGER SYSTEM

If we are to consider problem behavior as part of a system, we must also consider the supervisor's handling of problem behavior in terms of an even larger system. This larger system is made up of the employee's co-workers and the supervisor's co-workers. How an individual supervisor handles an incident is going to affect the attitudes and values of other employees as well. They will see, hear, and respond to the supervisor's actions just as the problem employee will. Further, other employees will judge the supervisor's fairness in dealing with their co-worker. This perception of fairness, subject as it is to interpretation and misunderstanding, will have an impact on whether or not they (the other employee) create later problems for the supervisor.

CAN ATTITUDES
BE CHANGED?

As we have seen, our values and attitudes take considerable time to form, and as they form, they are constantly being changed. The question might be better put: Can a supervisor change an employee's attitudes?

The answer is yes, but the direction and amount of change is not known or controlled. When a supervisor responds to any employee behavior (good or bad), the aftermath is an input to the employee's value system. He then operates on values that include this new aftermath information. *How* the employee operates (behaves) is not known. Even a seemingly appropriate, compassionate supervisory response may result in future problem behavior. Obviously, we assume that if a supervisor repeatedly responds to problem behavior in a positive way, the employee's attitudes will change. At the very least, we hope the employee's behavior will change. However, hoping is all we can do about an employee's attitude. It will change, but we can never be sure in what direction.

This should not imply that we're dealing with a hopeless situation. In the workplace, all that really matters is the employee's behavior, not his attitudes. Sure, the attitudes control the behavior, but they do so in many ways. Let's look at an example, making assumptions about the employee's attitudes based on what we know of the employee's behavior.

Employee Behavior	*Employee Attitude*
Employee insults good customer.	Employee does not care about the store's reputation with customers; store's reputation is irrelevant to employee's welfare.

Supervisor Response:
Supervisor reprimands employee. Threatens to fire employee if this sort of behavior happens again. Reminds employee that without customers, there would be no jobs.

Employee Behavior	*Employee Attitude*
Employee treats next customers courteously, with care, and according to company policy.	Employee understands importance of customers, wants to do a good job, and be liked by customers.

This simple example seems to suggest that the supervisor's reaction changed attitudes, resulting in more appropriate employee behavior. However, an alternate "attitude" might be:

Employee Behavior	*Employee Attitude*
Employee treats next customers courteously, with care, and according to company policy.	Employee needs, wants job. Fear of losing job means a change in behavior is necessary. Employee still feels the same about the store's reputation with customers.

Supervisors should take whatever actions are appropriate in dealing with problem employees. They should consider their own reactions as part of a continuing system of behavior, and they should try to gradually change and shape employee attitudes so that more productive behavior will result. In this chapter, our concern has been to identify behavior as a system. In later chapters, we will look at such related topics as motivation, performance, appraisal, and conflict management. We will also examine the role of personality—yours and the employee's—in handling problem behavior.

SOLUTION TO THE NINE-DOT SQUARE

As you can see, this puzzle cannot be solved by remaining within the square formed by the arrangement of the nine dots. It is only when we break out of these self-imposed boundaries that a solution is possible (Figure 7). It is often the same with problem behavior—the limitations, restrictions, and conditions we assume are there may have been put there by ourselves. They can be removed the same way.

FIGURE 7.

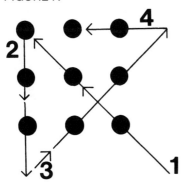

8

Using Persuasion To Change Problem Behavior

As managers interested in changing problem behavior, we constantly negotiate, persuade, and sell. We sell ideas, policies, behaviors—and ourselves. To persuade effectively, we must use all of the persuasive resources at our command. In this chapter, we'll look at some of these resources.

AVOIDING THE POWER STRUGGLE

When we communicate, we do so on two different levels.[1] The *content* level of communication deals with the subject, product, topic, or problem that concerns us at a particular time. We usually think of communication problems developing because two people can't agree on the content of a particular message. In a persuasion situation, therefore, a power struggle develops because they can't agree about who is responsible for what, or they can't agree with each other's definition of the problem, or they can't agree on the merits of a specific product. There are situations where this is true, but most experts on persuasion feel that real communication difficulties develop not in the content part of a sales encounter, but in the relationship part of the encounter. The *relationship* level of communication involves the way two individuals themselves define their relationship. When we accept the ideas, products, or "sales pitches" of persuasion transaction, the relationship between the persuader (the seller) and the person being persuaded (the buyer) is determined in advance. In all selling situations, the buyer is one-up over the seller because the buyer can pull out of the transaction at any time. In some persuasion situations, a power struggle develops when the seller attempts to take the upper hand and gain control over the buyer. This can be seen in the use of such phrases as "you must" and "you should." It can also be seen when the seller uses a buyer's questions as a chance to take charge. For example, if you're trying to persuade your boss about an idea you think will save your firm money, you're the seller, he or she is the buyer. If the boss asks, "What are the problems you see in such an approach?" you could respond with a simple list of potential problems, perhaps with your assessment of how these problems can be solved. In this case, the boss's question is an invitation to move from the "one-down position" and to communicate as an equal. Your reasoned and direct response shows that you accept the offer to communicate as equals. In transactional analysis, we'd call this a complimentary transaction, one adult to another. However, you could respond to the boss's simple question about potential problems by citing grand and elaborate claims, broad dismissals of any problems, and so on. For example,

BOSS: "What are the problems you see in such an approach?"
YOU: "Hey, not to worry, boss! I've thought through every angle, figured every catch, and there's absolutely no problem at all. Trust me, boss, this is a sure-fire, 100 percent success idea that can put this company on the map . . ."

If this sounds like high pressure, you're right. The employee (you) hasn't heard the question as a question or an opportunity to talk as equals. He views the question as a perfect chance to take control of the boss. If the boss accepts the takeover attempt, there will be no power struggle, although there may be some resentment over the high-pressure tactics. However, when dealing with the boss, there's more involved than just the roles of buyer and seller. There's also the role relationship of boss and employee, and in this relationship the boss is clearly on top. Because of this second relationship, there's a much greater chance for a power struggle to develop, especially when the seller (the employee) fights for the upper hand.

Consider another case in which the relationships aren't quite so clear. Suppose you are trying to motivate or persuade an employee to do something, to accept your idea, or to behave in a particular way. As the boss, you can order the employee to buy, but let's assume that you feel such an exercise of managerial power is unwise. Therefore, you decide to persuade, and in so doing, you again become the "seller" (one-down) communicating with the "buyer," who's one-up. Although this is a crossed transaction, no major problems will develop as long as you keep in mind that the buyer-seller relationship takes precedence over the employee-employer relationship. As the seller, you must listen for the buyer's real needs, for the doubts and uncertainties the buyer feels about your proposition. You'll also be listening for signals about changes in the relationship. Some of these signals include the following examples:

EMPLOYEE (BUYER): "Could you tell me more about _____?"
"I'm concerned about the _____."

These direct questions suggest that the buyer is looking for straight answers. Your best response is to give those straight answers. In the process, you're responding to the relationship signals and communicating as equals. No power struggle is involved.

EMPLOYEE (BUYER): "We've had some real problems with similar ideas. It won't work this time!"

Here, the employee is suggesting that she wishes to remain in the dominant position and that your persuasive argument needs some more support before a position of equal communication is appropriate. Often, this is the point at which bosses try to overcome their one-down position by reverting to the argument, "Look here, I'm the boss, and you do what I say!" which is really no argument at all. Instead of working within the relationship of buyer and seller, the boss tries to change the relationship to one in which she is clearly on top. The employee is then put in the position of having to either go along with the boss (in which case motivation has been replaced with force) or resist the boss. Because the boss holds many other "cards," such as poor work assignments, firing or disciplining, or simply displeasure, the employee will probably find it difficult to resist. However, when this change in positions does take place, the employee is put on notice that the boss wants to motivate and persuade as long as the employee goes along with the boss's wishes. In the long run, this will not create a motivating climate.

EMPLOYEE (BUYER): "You make a good case, boss. Since you're more experienced than I am in these things, I'll go along with your judgment."

In this situation, the employee (or buyer) is saying that she accepts the boss's expertise and is willing to reverse the roles and let the boss resume the dominant position. This is similar to the way most of us respond to medical advice from a doctor. As "buyers" of medical advice, we can accept or reject what the doctor tells us we should do. However, recognizing that the doctor has the professional expertise that we don't have, most of us are willing to trust the doctor to tell us what to do. Yet even doctors find that they are more successful in selling a particular kind of treatment or medical solution when they assume the "seller" role rather than the dominant "expert" role.

Although we've been suggesting that successful persuasion involves listening and responding to the relationship messages that others send us, as well as accepting the one-down position of the seller or persuader, we are not suggesting that to persuade you can't be aggressive. When you listen and respond to comments about the relationship and communicate as equals in the transaction, you can aggressively present your points of view. If you've done your homework before trying to persuade, you'll have the best answers to each of the buyer's objections already at hand. As long as you resist the temptation to respond to questions with a one-upper, you'll be able to present your strong and valid arguments and more than likely avoid the power struggle that gets in the way of your primary goal, which is to persuade the buyer to buy.

There are techniques that can help you become a more successful persuader. In our chapters on meetings, oral communication, body messages, and others, we've explored many of these techniques. In the next section, let's review them in one place and tie them specifically into the objective of getting your points across effectively.

DO'S AND DON'TS
OF SUCCESSFUL PERSUASION

In addition to the relationship messages of communication and the importance of listening and responding to these messages, there are some techniques that you can use to become a more effective persuader.

When persuading, be sure to use constant and direct eye contact, without staring at the individual. Keep your eyes frank and direct, but not cold and expressionless, and try to watch for subtle changes in the buyer's eyes, such as pupil dilation or increased blinking. These signals may indicate that the buyer's emotional state is changing and that you should "go for a close" or summarize and complete your presentation. Also, watch for and evaluate facial expressions for similar signs.

Keep your voice controlled, low but well modulated, and above all keep your voice relaxed. In a perfume commercial, the message suggests that you should "whisper if you want to get his attention." Whispering may not be an appropriate managerial communication strategy, but changes in the tone and level of your voice will accomplish the same thing. When you lower your voice, you can often see the listeners moving in toward you, to better hear what you're saying. You keep them from focusing on your monotone voice by raising and lowering it. If the person with whom you're talking has a hearing problem and clearly wants you to speak up, don't lower your voice too far, or you'll lose more than her attention. Women should try to avoid the high voice ranges, as their voices tend to get shrill when excessively raised. Both men and women sound demanding when their voices are too high, but soft and wavering voices should also be avoided as too passive and nonauthoritarian.

When persuading, keep your body as still as possible, thrust slightly forward. When seated, keep your hands in sight, but not folded across your chest or behind your head. Don't rock or swivel in your chair. Keep both feet firmly and flatly on the floor. Crossed legs tend to create more barriers and may look sloppy.

When standing, maintain a balanced stance, erect but not rigid. Avoid "storking" (standing on one foot with the other tucked behind your leg and your foot on the tip), leaning, or stooping. Try to avoid excessive head nods. All can be interpreted by your buyer as signs of weakness. However, do remember the positive effects of occasional and aggressive signals, such as hands on the hips, arms folded tightly across the chest, or feet wide apart. These are often viewed by buyers as domineering signals, and they can be interpreted as attempts by the persuader (you) to take a dominant, one-up position in the transaction.

The amount of hand movement we use is controlled by factors over which we have little control. In general, it's wise to avoid excessive hand fluttering, although some hand movement is natural and effective as a means of emphasizing your points. When persuading, avoid playing with beards, moustaches, or hair. Avoid clenched fists, finger pointing, and table pounding. All these gestures can and are frequently interpreted by employees as dominance gestures and are, therefore, seen as threats to the buyer's one-up position.

In general, your persuasive messages will be more successful when you convey to your employees a sense of competence, self-assurance, and strength. Combine this with an attitude that you really care about the employee and his problems and that your proposals or plans are aimed at satisfying the major needs of your buyer. Unless you are with intimates, avoid sarcasm or flippancy when trying to persuade, as these messages often imply an equality position that usually is not present in a persuasion transaction, even after the sale is complete. Don't overdo "superiority" messages or exaggerated shows of strength or knowledge, although you're wise not to shy away from them either. In the final analysis, a strong content and a strong relationship message is the best communication strategy for successful persuasion.

Personalize Your Appeal

According to most persuasion studies, those having the most success as persuaders are those who tailor their persuasive appeals to the specific needs of the person being persuaded.[2] Thus, you're better off avoiding a standard "line" or appeal when trying to persuade. Doing so makes about as much sense as a shoe store stocking all size nine shoes because the average size of their customers' feet is size nine. Some people are susceptible to direct appeals, and others must be persuaded using roundabout methods. As one successful persuader has suggested, "standard pitches usually result in standard results, and they are often 'no sale.' " We respond best to appeals and persuasive messages aimed directly at our needs.

Listen for Needs,
Then Respond

Persuasion is not simply a matter of talking to someone about the many benefits, advantages, and features of your idea or point of view. Too often, this becomes a high-pressure situation, in which a take-charge attitude is used by the persuader in an attempt to overcome any and all objections. As we have already seen, a major problem with this approach is that it can easily turn off the person being persuaded. Instead of high pressure, try to listen for needs and hidden problems and objections. Use questions to probe the person being persuaded, to learn what may be on his mind. Once you have a clearer idea of the feelings and attitudes of your buyer, you'll be in a better position to make a successful persuasive appeal.

Watch Your
Own Credibility

Doctors, tax advisers, attorneys, and others with a lot of built-in credibility don't have a lot of trouble with persuasion, at least not in terms of their professional advice. The reason for this is that the success one enjoys in persuasion is directly related to his credibility. On the other hand, used-car salesmen, door-to-door roofing salesmen, and others with low credibility usually have more difficulty getting people to buy their ideas and products. Since your personal reputation plays such an important role in your success as a persuader, it's an advantage to maintain a credible reputation with your employees and avoid a "credibility gap." Although personal credibility and integrity are important in persuasion, this is not the only kind of credibility you have going for you. As a manager of a professional organization, you also have the credibility of your organization and your position working for you. As a representative of your facility, you command considerable authority and prestige. Use it. Of course, as your relationship with a client or employee progresses, the credibility and reputation of your organization becomes secondary to the reliability, honesty, and trust the individual expects from you.

The value of personal integrity in persuasion is directly related to the "high-pressure–low-pressure" issue we discussed earlier. Often high-pressure persuaders find themselves making exaggerated claims or promises for themselves or their points of view. They tend to bend the truth and may feel that anything to make the "sale" or convince the other person is an acceptable part of the persuasion process. But if you want to develop a credible ongoing employee (or patient) relationship, in which your reputation is an asset instead of a liability, such tactics won't work.

Make Your Conclusions Clear

A common misunderstanding in persuasion is that people are much more likely to accept conclusions if they develop them themselves. Yet, according to the latest research on persuasion, people are more likely to change their opinions in the direction you desire when you give them a clear indication what that direction is. Without such signals, you can't be sure your persuasive efforts will yield the results you desire.

This advice does not mean that you should force others to accept your ideas. Any acceptance you get from this strategy is apt to be a response to the pressure and not to the value of your idea or the persuasiveness of your logic. Gentle guidance and a clear but subtle indication of your position is the best bet.

The Three-Martini Lunch

Despite the efforts of some legislators to do away with business entertainment tax deductions, there is strong research to suggest that pleasant forms of distraction can help in a persuasive appeal. This is perhaps why you'll find more models in bathing suits than boats at boat shows, or why well-designed store displays seem to encourage sales. Still, if the pleasant distraction becomes too much of a distraction you'll have difficulty getting someone's attention long enough to make your position clear. There is real power in pleasant distraction that can actually help your employee focus her attention on your idea or proposal. In the normal work environment, employees are subjected to all sorts of pressures and distractions, and often it is necessary for them to "shift gears" and completely ignore your persuasive message. You find yourself repeating the same persuasive argument several times, with less success each time. Pleasant distractions need not always be synonymous with the fabled three-martini lunch. They can also include doing your persuading in a comfortable location, giving compliments on the other person's attire or their performance on a recent project or difficult assignment, or telling a funny story as a "tension breaker" to put the other person at ease.

Resist the temptation to use pleasant distractions as a substitute for a well-planned and well-executed persuasive appeal. Such distractions may turn the tide on marginal appeals, but they rarely do much for really poor ideas.

Encourage Involvement and Participation

Persuasion seems to work best when the buyer has an opportunity to get involved with an idea or an approach. Passive participation, such as the seller using rhetorical questions, is useful, although active participation is much better. Encourage discussion, wait for comments and questions, and give the person being persuaded every chance to become a part of the process.

This same advice also extends to group participation. When dealing with a group of employees, try to focus your appeal and your strongest arguments directly at the group members you feel are the opinion leaders. Encourage the group to discuss all aspects of the proposal you're making, but be sure that you remain in control and that you give a clear picture of the goal you want to achieve. Keep in mind that our attitudes and opinions are strongly influenced by the group to which we belong or would like to belong. By appealing to these desires for group acceptance and identification, you can make your job as persuader much easier. When working to get people involved in a persuasive appeal, there's another factor to be considered.

People tend to be much more resistant to changing ideas and positions that they have publicly expressed (even to you) than they are to ideas or positions they hold privately. Thus, although open discussion is useful for encouraging participation, be careful about a premature public statement of a person's position until you're reasonably sure he is leaning your way. For example, suppose you are trying to persuade your work group to accept a new scheduling plan for their work hours. A full discussion of the merits of your proposal is useful, but if too many of the opinion leaders in the group come out against your proposal, they (and their fellow group members) will be far less likely to change their positions later, even if you present some powerful and persuasive arguments. A public commitment is difficult for most of us to back away from, since we may feel that doing so will make us lose face, or appear wishy-washy. Thus, when persuading, your preparation and analysis of the "buyer's" real needs, objections, and positions should guide you in deciding when to go for a public disclosure of feelings or a public commitment of position.

Although this advice is useful in all persuasion situations, it is clearly a life-or-death matter in situations where terrorists take and hold hostages. Law enforcement people dislike detailed television and media coverage of such situations because it tends to harden positions on both sides. Dr. Robert Shellow, the principal social scientist on the

National Advisory Committee on Social Disorders, suggests that "the more a situation becomes public, the more it loses fluidity. It's like labor negotiations or politics. The President and the Congress can argue in private and make progress—each side giving, each taking. But once the press reports where each stands, the positions are set in stone."[3] The same premise of private counsel on issues and positions until some agreement can be reached was behind the Middle-East peace conference between Carter of the United States, Sadat of Egypt, and Begin of Israel in September 1978. As in all persuasion situations, premature disclosure of a position or attitude contrary to yours can lead to "no sale." Of course, once the buyer's attitude has been moved to your point of view, disclosure can seal the commitment.

One Side
or Both Sides?

Among persuasion experts, there is a difference of opinion about the relative value of presenting one side or both sides of an agreement. The *one-side position* is that you will weaken your argument by bringing up contrary facts. You run the risk of confusing the person being persuaded, and you may inadvertantly talk yourself out of a sale. By concentrating on *your* side of an argument or issue, you avoid distractions and keep your attention and your employee's firmly on the goal you want to reach.

The *both-sides position* suggests that people are usually aware of both sides, anyway. By ignoring the opposing side, you may insult the person you're trying to persuade by suggesting that you feel he is uninformed and can be hoodwinked. Also, proponents of this position, suggest that when you get on a one-sided argument, there's more tendency to exaggerate and overstate your position. By airing both sides, you create some balance in your persuasive argument and in effect keep yourself under control.

Your choice about presenting one or both sides of an argument is also related to the attitudes and feelings the other person has about the situation. If you've discovered that the person you're trying to persuade is generally in favor of your position, it's usually best to present only your side of the story. However, if the other person is generally opposed or hostile to your position or idea, you must explore both sides, raising objections against both sides and generally presenting a balanced picture.

Facts Don't Always
"Speak for Themselves"

Many persuaders not only shun high-pressure tactics, they also feel that facts or information fairly presented are all that's necessary to persuade. Certainly this is sometimes true, but information alone does not change attitudes or opinions or persuade people. When actively persuading, draw a thread through your facts. Show how those facts directly benefit the employee being persuaded and how his needs will be satisfied by using your suggestion. Don't confuse low-pressure or no-pressure persuading with passively presenting information and then stepping back.

Sandwich Bad News,
Highlight Good News

When making a persuasive appeal, remember that facts presented at the beginning or end of a presentation are highlighted and are far more likely to be remembered than the same facts in the middle of a presentation. Try an experiment. Look at the following list of three-letter "words" for ten seconds, then cover the list with your hand and read the instructions below:

DZR
ENM
QKT
SRP
KNP
CMS
LJX

Now, without looking at the list, see how many of the seven items you can reproduce. If you're like most people, you remember the first two or three items. However, the items in the middle just don't seem to be there.

In rumor transmission, the "law of primacy" is that first and last facts are more likely to stay in a rumor and have more impact on each listener than middle facts. Knowing this aspect of perception can work two ways. When you're trying to persuade someone to accept an idea, you'll probably have several points or persuasive items to use in your argument. If you've done your "prepersuasion planning," you should have an idea of which of your points will be most appealing to your "buyer." To give these points the attention and emphasis they deserve, put them first, to grab your listener's interest. Doing so, it's possible that you'll only need one point to convince him about your proposal. For example, "If you accept this new idea, you'll find you have more time to yourself." If the main need of your employee is more time, you don't need to say much more. You probably have him persuaded. When you put your key or "clinching" point at the end, you may have to do more talking, but you can slowly build toward your main point, using it as the final factor in your persuasive appeal.

Although good news and positive persuasive arguments should be put at the start or end of a persuasion transaction to give them emphasis, bad news messages of factors detracting from your persuasive appeal should appear in the middle of your presentation. This is known as the sandwiching effect, putting bad news in between two positive or good-news statements. Although a discussion of sandwiching and the handling of bad news messages is beyond our scope in this chapter, it is an interesting offshoot of the persuasive law of primacy.

Repeat, Repeat, Repeat

Like limestone, granite, or your memory before an exam, the persuasive effects of a message will wear away in time. The well-documented learning curve is based on the notion that only 10 to 15 percent of a once-heard message will be remembered for any amount of time, and slightly higher proportions of the message will be remembered after successive repetitions. Yet, too often, we put together a well-balanced persuasive message, present it to someone once, and then assume the message is remembered. Managers are constantly making such statements as, "I told so-and-so (the "buying employee") about the new schedule last week, and she said she'd think about it. There's no sense going back over the same ground again. When she's ready, she'll come around." This is sheer nonsense. Listen to television commercials. In a thirty-second spot they will say or show the product's name many times. Each repetition helps secure that name in the consumer's mind. A good public speaker uses the "rule of three" ("tell 'em what you're gonna say, say it, then tell 'em what you told 'em!") to reinforce her message. The same principle applies in education, where you may study the "hygienic theory of motivation" or the "sender-message-receiver model of communication" or the "metabolic distress curve" in several different college courses. You may not like or agree with the concept, but you sure will remember it.

Repetition of a persuasive message helps ward off the effects of time. Many persuaders find that they can improve their persuasive results by focusing on one or two persuasive points and then repeating those points in many ways over an extended period of time. Assuming that "once is enough" is foolish, and it can undermine an otherwise well-planned and well-executed persuasive message.

Don't Overdo the Dramatic

Some people feel that really sensational or dramatic appeals are the best way to produce a long-term attitude or opinion change or to persuade someone not presently in favor of "buying." Apparently using this approach, some terrorists use dramatic public happenings to focus on their cause and thereby change public opinion and bring in "converts." But research into persuasion and attitude change suggests just the opposite. The most sensational of dramatic forms of persuasion can often be the least effective of all appeals in producing significant attitude change, especially over a long period of time.

Know How to Get a Commitment

The most difficult job in a persuasive appeal is knowing when and how to get a commitment. This means asking the person being persuaded to express an opinion or make a commitment toward the idea or proposal you're advocating. In all forms of persuasion, it is the moment of truth.

Knowing when to close is a matter of listening for subtle signals from the employee. A long period of silence, a lowering of the voice, fewer questions, a body posture of "leaning back," a dilation of the pupils of the eyes—all can be signals that it's time to close the persuasive encounter and ask for the "sale." Knowing when to close takes time and experience with persuasion, and even expert persuaders agree that it develops as you do more and more persuading.

When reaching this point in a persuasive conversation, don't leave the employee in a state of indecision. If it's at all possible, get some commitment—however small—in order to have an opening later if a repeat discussion is necessary. Also, don't try to rush a person toward a decision. Few of us can use high pressure in a way that doesn't appear to be high pressure, and rushing or pressing for a decision is often taken as a form of high pressure in persuasion.

Convey a positive outlook, and avoid weak statements such as "I hope you'll think about what I've said." *If, hope, maybe,* and *I think* are all weakness words, and they rarely help a persuasive message. Your positive outlook should also extend to your body language and facial expressions. Look interested in the other person, and don't show signs of disappointment or rejection if you're turned down. After all, they are rejecting your idea or proposal, but they're not rejecting *you*. If you look dejected or disinterested at closing time, you may lose this "sale," and you may also make the next persuasion attempt even less successful.

Don't try to get a commitment from the person you're trying to persuade until all his objections and questions have been answered. When you ignore, refuse to answer, or gloss over questions, you again appear high pressured. We often say, "It's not what you say that counts, it's what you don't say." In persuasion, evasion by the persuader often translates into high pressure, and that seldom works.

Know When to Quit

In persuasion, a cardinal rule is to "say our piece and shut up!" Too often a good persuasive message is ruined because the persuader didn't know when to quit. Instead of making the best point last and then stopping to let the other person think and respond, they keep on going. They raise new issues, rehash points that don't need rehashing, and generally get in the way of their own message. This also applies to written persuasive messages. Writers can put together a beautiful written appeal that is well organized, with everything leading up to the "clincher" at the end, and then keep on going page after page. The listener gets bored and tunes out; the reader simply skips over sections or just stops reading. Either way, too much message is worse than too little, and it usually doesn't persuade.

When you've made your last point, stop and wait. Look at the other person as though you're interested in responding to objections or questions, but don't pester him with more facts. If it seems appropriate, ask if he has any feelings about what you've said and then give him a chance to express those feelings. If your persuasive message was well planned and well delivered, it deserves to be treated with respect by you *and* the person receiving it.

Plan Your Work
and Work Your Plan

We've suggested a number of factors that are important in persuasion. Some may be common sense, others may not be familiar at all. All are based on expert research into persuasion, motivation, and attitude change. To use them in any sort of persuasive appeal, plan in advance what you are going to do and then follow through on those plans. If planning is important as a basic management function, it is surely as important as a part of successful persuasion.

Effective persuasion is not complicated or mysterious. It is a combination of common sense and applied research, and it is a simple two-step process. When trying to persuade, analyze the person you're persuading and determine his real needs. Second, listen and respond when it's appropriate by making your presentation fit those needs. When your persuasive appeal is oriented toward your employee, it will be as a sign of genuine interest in that individual. Developing such a "you" orientation toward others can make you a more persuasive manager.

9

Managing
Interpersonal Conflict

Conflict and management go hand in hand.[1] Throughout a typical day, you find yourself in a wide variety of conflicts and potential conflicts with employees, competitors, friends, and family. The very word *conflict* suggests negative or unproductive behavior. We associate conflict with "battle," "hostility," or "warfare," and there is good and ample reason for such feelings. Yet conflict is not always a negative outcome of organizational behavior. Creative conflict over differences in business policies or operations can result in better ideas and greater profits. Within an organization, properly managed conflict can help produce more member interest in the organization's activities. It can keep the staff on their toes and aware of their mission to serve client or customer needs. Creative conflict can also bring about useful change in organizations. Managers often comment, "If we didn't have some occasional conflict in my department, I'd have to create some just to keep my blood moving." A common follow-up comment is, "Luckily, my people feel the same way because they seem to come up with a new conflict every week."

WHAT IS CONFLICT?

Conflict is any situation in which the goals, methods, aims, or objectives of two or more parties are in opposition. Conflict also is a situation when potential solutions appear to be mutually exclusive. One solution prevents any other. Many conflicts arise over the allocation of scarce resources. If one department wants to spend money for new equipment and another is pushing for staff development funding, a conflict is apt to occur over spending the firm's limited available money. The departments appear to have mutually exclusive goals. A major education program means little or no funding for new equipment, and vice versa. Conflicts may develop over performance standards, location of meetings, the management's handling of the carpet in the office. Although some of these conflicts have a major impact on a group or department, and others seem trivial, none can be completely ignored for very long.

Some conflicts are caused by one person's ignorance of another person's position. A manager reads a statement issued by the training director and interprets the statement in a negative way. Yet, on further examination, both people want the same things. Their conflict stems from a problem with semantics and can be handled by better communication. For this reason, communication is often cited as a major strategy for managing conflict. This is good advice *if* the parties are ignorant of each other's similar position. In this case, better communication can help. But suppose two parties in a conflict begin to communicate and discover that they are, in fact, miles apart. In this interaction, they also discover just how strongly the other person feels about her position. Armed with this new and more accurate information, the battle lines are hardened, and the conflict intensifies. Worse still is the situation where two parties are in *apparent agreement* on every detail except one. To resolve the remaining barriers to total agreement, they begin to communicate more about their respective positions, and in doing so, they may discover that what they thought was agreement was really ignorance of each other's conflicting position. Now the battle begins.

In general, good open communication is better than poor or nonexistent communication, but don't be misled into believing that better communication automatically leads to reduced conflict.

RESOLVE OR MANAGE CONFLICT?

Our usual goal is to resolve a conflict and get on with productive activity. When conflict is resolved, it goes away and is no longer a concern. Yet few conflicts are really resolved with no trace of aftermath. In situations where a vote or consensus ends the conflict, one person or group wins, another loses. In a democratic system, the losing side usually gets behind the winner and the conflict is resolved. But do losers always forget their differences and join hands in a spirit of solidarity? More often, there is some residual resentment to any conflict "resolution."

The loser is apt to feel that "they beat me this time, but I'm not through yet. I'll go along for appearances and wait for another time to make my move." This loser attitude of "don't get mad, get even" is the reason why few win-lose conflicts can be resolved permanently.

"Conflict resolution" implies a final solution—an end to a particular problem. Yet throughout history the resolution of one conflict actually led to later conflicts. The Treaty of Versailles ended World War I, yet many historians feel that the treaty's conditions and stipulations created the springboard for Hitler and World War II. In the same way, the solution to the conflict over the carpet color in a department or the allocation of raise money may leave a "loser" unwilling to rest until he has "showed 'em they can't treat me that way!"

The aftermath of any conflict sets the stage for future conflicts. Conflict is not a series of isolated events. It is a process that can be effectively managed, but rarely resolved.

Who is to blame? Placing blame is an attempt to find a starting place for a conflict and thereby identify "who's right." This is a process, and the start cannot be pinpointed by simply repeating the effects. In the same sense, the history of a present conflict between one manager and another cannot be easily traced to a single event, nor is the conflict likely to cease because the "blame" has been identified.

The challenge in handling conflict is to behave in a way that will minimize the damaging effects of the present conflict while minimizing the possibility for future conflicts. Robert Blake and Jane Mouton identified several commonly used strategies for managing conflict. Each of these strategies have long-range and short-range possibilities. Each conflict management strategy has certain aftermath that managers need to consider.

Compromise

The role of compromise in conflict resolution or management is interesting. Often we try to use compromise to resolve a conflict. Both parties agree that they can't get everything they want, and they settle for something instead of nothing. A well-designed compromise that benefits both parties and reduces hostility is an effective way to manage conflict, although a compromise does not guarantee that future conflicts will not develop. Suppose there is a conflict over who will manage a new project. A compromise is reached, where one person gets the job and the other person agrees to a later assignment on a later project in return for some concessions on operating rules controlling the new project. The bargain is struck; the assignment is made. Is this the end of a conflict?

What happens if supporters of the other person feel that their candidate "sold out"? Will the compromise hold if the person who agreed to make concessions later feels that the "winner" is reneging on her commitments? Will the person who "won" follow through with her commitments if she feels the presence of the "strong second" person as a challenge to her authority?

When bargaining is used as a strategy for managing conflict, there is always a danger that the bargain will come unstuck and that the conflict will flare again. If each party to a bargain trusts the other, the compromise may hold. If there is a strong third party involved, such as an arbitrator or respected statesman, he may be able to keep the parties faithful to their bargain. Still, the very nature of a bargain is that each party wins some and loses some. The perception of loss can be an important breeding ground for future conflicts. A compromise on budget allocations may produce "watchdogs" on each side who are looking for apparent violations in the compromise while at the same time looking for ways to tilt a fifty-fifty compromise to a sixty-forty out-come—with their side getting the 60 percent.

"Do It My Way, or Else."

This is a win-lose strategy. The winner has more power and can force the loser to accept whatever solution the winner imposes. In sports, a major defeat leads to the cry "wait till next year." In other situations, it may lead to the cry, "wait till next time" or "wait till he wants help getting that plan moving and see how much he gets out of us!" A forced solution of a conflict can lead to the loser desiring to get even. It can motivate losers to resist or even sabotage the winner's positions and actions. The loss of self-esteem or "face" may lead to repercussions. At best, a forced solution gets losers' cooperation at "gunpoint," with little or no enthusiasm for or commitment to the winning side. A succession of losses can stifle creativity, leading to an unresponsive organization. The attitude is, "If he's so smart all the time, let him figure this one out by himself. He'll just shoot down anything I say anyway."

One Big Happy Family

In some conflicts, we respond by pointing to the futility of an open battle and instead suppress the conflict in hopes it will go away. Smoothing over a conflict may involve getting the warring parties to lower their public voices, shake hands, and issue joint statements pledging mutual love for each other or the company. This strategy is based on the assumption that "emphasizing the positive" will defuse a conflict and make it go away. In the short run, smoothing may actually work, in the same way a cease-fire stops the battlefield shooting, but smoothing does little to get at or handle the causes of a conflict, and it rarely leads to a long-term solution. It calls for stalling, in hopes that "things will change" and the need for a battle will cease. Taken at its extreme, smoothing becomes appeasement, and world history shows the dismal record of appeasement as a means of resolving conflict.

I Don't Want to Talk about It

While bargaining, forcing, and smoothing all do *something* about a conflict, withdrawal is doing *nothing* about it. Ignoring a conflict makes it go away to the same extent that an ostrich with its head in the sand makes an enemy disappear. Yet there are situations where even withdrawal can be useful in managing a conflict episode. At a meeting, one participant is very upset, shouting and raving that the manager and his cronies are conspiring to make the progressives look bad. Tempers are heated, facts become opinions, and logic turns to gut-level reactions. Continuing to argue the merits of various positions would be futile and could even lead to remarks in the heat of battle that would damage the group's ability to govern. In this situation, forcing a vote or smoothing over the differences in the group may lead to further trouble. When forced to go in an unacceptable direction, the "losers" may attempt to sabotage the decision. They can withhold information or support, or they can actively subvert the majority's efforts. Smoothing may leave both sides feeling they've been had, or have been given the "treatment," which can build into smoldering resentment. Withdrawal or avoidance is useful because you remove the *opportunity* to continue fighting. Adjourn the meeting. Walk out. Change the subject abruptly or diplomatically, or refuse to comment in any way until tempers have cooled.

Too much withdrawal or withdrawal for too long is poor leadership. In the vacuum, cliques will form and strengthen, and positions will harden. Nonleaders may attempt a coup to take over, and the longer withdrawal from a conflict continues, the more likely their efforts will be to succeed.

Withdrawing or avoiding a battle is an effective short-run ploy. It is used to gain an advantage by allowing for a better time, place, or situation for a confrontation. It can also be useful when you are facing several problems at once. Trying to handle them all can drain your energy and reduce your effectiveness and that of your staff. Instead of fighting four fires at once, you may select the two most critical and consciously ignore the other two. You minimize the total damage from the four. Still, remember that the conflicts you consciously ignored because they seemed less important may develop into major controversies because of this inattention.

Optimizing Conflict

All the strategies we usually associate with conflict have advantages and disadvantages. The common factor in all of them is the potential for future conflict, the so-called latent conflict. In the short run, they may help you to resolve the immediate battle, but at some long-run cost. The best overall strategy for long-run conflict management is *optimizing* or *confrontation*. It involves changing the focus of a conflict away from blame, starting points, causes, and specific solutions and toward an overall remedy for the problem. It is often called a *problem-solving* strategy because it requires the participants to seek common points of agreement, not as a compromise solution, but as a basis for a comprehensive solution to a problem. Optimizing produces no losers and thus minimizes the aftermath of a present conflict. It does not mean that all parties to a conflict get everything they wanted. It does mean that all parties commit themselves to an optimal solution instead of grudgingly agreeing to a "half-a-loaf" compromise while waiting for a chance to "get it all."

Following are eight guides to managing conflict through optimizing or problem-solving:

1. *Direct confrontation between opposing parties is essential.* This is the key element in an optimizing strategy. The opposing sides must be willing to face each other (and each other's ideas) head-on. There's no opportunity for ducking side issues, smiling to make things appear friendly, or lining up bargaining chips for later. Confrontation in a meeting may lead to the following dialogue:

YOU: "Harry, we've both been letting off a lot of steam here, and frankly I'm worried about the effect on the company. I feel your comments on the proposal are actually potshots at me personally and that you're trying to make a grab for power. I don't mind telling you that scares me: not because you'll win or I'll lose, but what the battle may do to our competitive position. Tell me, Harry, how do you feel about me *personally?*"

HARRY: "Hey, I don't mean anything personally, Al. Look, I'm just as interested in the company as you are—maybe more. After all, I've been here fifteen years. I love this business, and I'm committed to the firm."

YOU: "Harry, everyone here appreciates you and your efforts. But you're ducking the issue. How do you feel about *me* as a *person?*"

HARRY: "Why, is it important?"

YOU: "If we can't confront each other honestly and openly about our feelings toward each other, those hidden feelings will just get in our way as we try to work out our problems. Listen, tell me how you feel—no holds barred—the goods *and* the bads. Fair enough?"

Obviously, this approach is dangerous, and full of risk. Harry may welcome the chance to let you have an earful about your shortcomings and alleged weaknesses. On the other hand, Harry may also respond with an honest assessment of his feelings toward you and your performance as manager. Direct confrontation on a person-to-person basis (rather than a position-to-position basis) is the way to begin managing conflict.

2. *Get personality feelings up front first.* In your first contact with your opponent, try to talk about how you feel about each other.

Conflicts are often heightened and solutions made more difficult because there is a "hidden agenda" in the conflict. People are conflicting over their relationship as well as the issue at hand, and the relationship conflict is the roadblock to agreement. It is also a major contributor to a destructive conflict aftermath.

When two political factions argue over a bond issue, they often do not dispute the public good and the merits of the bond-financed projects. What they are disputing is the question of who will be in charge at City Hall. Handling the power relationship is the key to managing the conflict, the actual issue is secondary. When a manager challenges a governing board's decision on the site for an upcoming meeting in Las Vegas, is the manager really arguing that she prefers Podunk for the meeting? Or is she trying to assert power over the board?

The personality issues rarely go away when a conflict is settled. Regardless of whether the bond issue passes or fails, regardless of the outcome of the "Anywhere but Podunk" controversy, personal feelings will remain, and they will become the basis for the next conflict. Successful conflict *management* aims at reducing the chance that future conflicts will arise by reducing hostility and damaging aftereffects. It is important to get the relationship or feeling aspects all out in the open first, before tackling the major issues. You won't necessarily change your opponent's feelings about you, but at least you'll be able to separate his feelings about *you* from his feelings about the issue being argued.

3. *Minimize status differences.* When confronting a conflict head-on, it's best to keep the opposing parties on a reasonably equal footing. In working out conflicts with and among your employees, status differences are important. Imagine sitting in your office behind your executive desk, Gucci-clad feet propped up on the desk, while an employee sprawls comfortably in a straight-backed chair, separated from your desk by your expensive Persian carpet. Can you communicate as equals and ignore the differences in your relative status?

A better approach is to find a neutral site for the confrontation. If your objective is to enforce your position, the status advantages are useful. However, this is *forcing* a conflict solution, not *optimizing*.

4. *Don't try to place blame.* In most conflicts, the participants spend a lot of time trying to shift the blame for the problem from one side to the other. If one side can successfully fix blame on the opponents, it's possible for them to "win" the conflict. In an optimizing strategy, fixing blame serves no useful purpose, and it should be avoided.

5. *Delay commitments to specific solutions.* When we try to solve a conflict, we often contribute to the difficulties by holding out for a specific solution. A better approach is to delay as long as possible committing yourself to a certain course of action. Too much of delay can give you the appearance of a poor leader, but a "tolerable" delay may help all participants in a conflict hold their options open and remain flexible about an ultimate optimal solution.

6. *Identify areas of mutual agreement.* An optimizing solution to a conflict is one that minimizes the aftereffects that lead to future conflicts. It is also an approach that focuses on an overall solution to a problem, rather than on a winner and a loser. To achieve this outcome, try to identify early in the confrontation the areas where all parties can agree. This is often called "commitment to superordinate goals." Simply put, it means focusing the attention of the fighting parties on some larger goals that they have in common. For example, in a conflict between factions in a group, members can always focus on the good of the firm. Both sides will readily agree that the company comes first, and that their position is best for the company. Rather than have everyone involved in the conflict agree that the firm comes first and then resume their fighting, keep the attention on the mutual goal as long as possible. When one side or the other starts to slip into a discussion of their favored solution, bring the discussion back to the larger mutual goals of both sides. When the parties in a conflict can evaluate their common goals and focus on how to achieve them instead of defending their predetermined positions, an optimal outcome to the conflict is possible.

7. *Emphasize mutual benefits.* When a natural disaster hits a community, the usual bases for conflict within the community disappear. The politics, skin colors, economic positions, and historical differences of the people in the community become unimportant. Restoring order and resuming life is the overall goal of everyone, and such a mutual benefit is possible only if past feelings and differences are put aside. A large American airline found itself facing a similarly dangerous position. Without some drastic cost cutting, they faced certain bankruptcy. Labor and management agreed that their mutual benefit was in cooperation instead of the usual hostility. Labor agreed to set aside some of its salary and benefit increases stipulated in the contract, and management agreed to a salary cut and a "no-layoff" policy. Working together, the difficulties were overcome. Yet each side had a right to enforce its position with legal action. The emphasis on mutual benefit made it possible to set aside the traditional management-labor conflict. Focusing mutual benefits is also an integral part of the problem-solving aspect of an optimizing strategy.

8. *Examine your own biases and feelings first.* Before confronting a conflict, take a close look at your own feelings and attitudes about your opponent and the conflict that confronts you. Knowing your attitudes may help you get them "up front" and thus keep them from interfering with a problem-oriented solution to the conflict.

ADAPT AND BE REALISTIC

When facing a conflict situation, realistically evaluate the participants, the stakes, and the setting. Determine how important the issue is to you, to your organization, and to your staff. Keep in mind that no single strategy works best in all situations. Remember too that confronting a conflict head-on may still result in a bargain between the warring parties. The goal is to minimize the aftereffects and keep conflicts manageable and productive.

Don't be a Pollyanna. Realistically, some conflicts cause permanent damage despite the best efforts of all concerned to minimize the aftermath. Think of conflict management as being similar to forest fire management. The forest service doesn't put out every fire and save every tree. If it is successful, it minimizes the damage from forest fires and keeps enough of the forest green to insure that there will be a need for a forest service. Remember, after a bad burn, new trees spring to life and the forest goes on. If you've done your best to manage conflicts in your organization, you'll still be in business and in control of the seeds of growth in your organization. You'll also develop a healthy attitude of creative conflict management.

10
Coaching
and Counseling
Problem Employees

Problem employees are a threat to any organization. Their less-than-desired performance results in missed goals, lower profits, and poorly done work. Their influence on other employees can reduce the overall organization's productivity. The managerial efforts devoted to monitoring and changing problem behavior take time that could otherwise be spent on productive activity. And the stress caused by having to counsel problem employees, and perhaps ultimately fire them, takes a toll on every manager confronted with the problem.[1]

Most negative information about an employee's performance is presented to the employee during some sort of *performance appraisal*. In many organizations, performance appraisal is a regular part of the employer-employee relationship. The manager uses a variety of forms and follows a prescribed procedure in communicating to the employee how she is doing and what is expected during the coming period. In other firms, performance appraisal is done haphazardly and only when there is a specific outbreak of problem behavior that must be attended to by the manager. Either way, the interaction between boss and subordinate over problem behavior can be extremely difficult. It is far easier to compliment an employee on her outstanding performance or to offer a raise or promotion than it is to offer criticism or counseling in a constructive and beneficial way. It is downright unpleasant to have to criticize an employee, or to inform the person that she will not be promoted, or to persuade someone that she should come to work on time—or else!

It is exactly this unpleasantness that Douglas McGregor had in mind when he noted the following:

> Managers are uncomfortable when they are put in the position of playing God. The respect we hold for the inherent value of the individual leaves us distressed when we take responsibility for judging the personal worth of a fellow man. Yet the conventional approach to performance appraisal forces us not only to make such judgments and to see them acted upon but also to communicate them to those we have judged. Small wonder we resist.[2]

Managers dislike giving bad news almost as much as subordinates dislike getting it. For this reason, employee appraisals are often avoided completely. The problem of vanishing appraisals is important to managers because the absence of feedback undermines the effectiveness of any motivation program.

One way managers avoid giving negative criticism is to tell all employees that they are performing well. If a manager rates 80 percent of his employees as good or outstanding, but only gives raises to 20 percent, there appears to be an enormous communication breakdown, at least from the subordinate's viewpoint. The subordinate has every reason to believe he will be rewarded, since he was told that he was performing well. When the reward doesn't come, distrust and bad feelings are sure to emerge. Even if animosity doesn't occur, the employee has no way of knowing how to improve, since the manager evaded his responsibility for giving accurate feedback. In the attempt to minimize the discomfort of both subordinate and superior, the superior may have created an even bigger problem of employee dissatisfaction. Thus, one of the main reasons for poor performance evaluations is a lack of managerial skill in handling difficult counseling situations.

Performance appraisals serve two purposes. (1) the planning for, monitoring of, and training of the subordinate and (2) the administration of salaries and rewards. Both are extremely important, and both put the manager into a classic role conflict. Can a manager be a friend, confidant, counselor, and trainer while still being the coach and the keeper of the purse strings? It's a difficult position because the manager can't be sure which role should get more attention and commitment. The situation poses alternatives from which each manager must make a choice. From a communication standpoint, the critical issue is which role employees perceive the manager to be emphasizing. The conflict between being a coach and being a counselor adds to the discomfort and conflict during the performance appraisal.

COUNSELING STRATEGIES

There are strategies for reducing the stress experienced by managers, thus enabling them to communicate with subordinates in a nondefense-provoking manner. Prescriptions for managerial behavior are often viewed suspiciously by supervisors and managers who realize that there is no single answer for all situations. Since many contingencies are involved, the following suggestions must be interpreted in light of one's own managerial setting. Although there is no definitive technique, these suggestions may be taken as guidelines and merged with your own managerial style, skills, and organizational constraints.

IDENTIFY THE BEHAVIORS
To achieve the desired performance from an employee, the employee must know exactly what is expected of him. The manager's responsibility is to provide the employee with a complete, precise, and clear understanding of the behaviors that are desired. This provides the subordinate with a greater appreciation of what is to be done and forces the manager to be more specific in his expectations and, there-

fore, more objective in his evaluations. Properly done, it can create a less defensive atmosphere between the superior and the subordinate.

If a manager tells a subordinate to "take care of that problem," there is a good chance the subordinate may not completely understand how he is to proceed, since many alternatives are available to him. On the other hand, if the manager tells the subordinate to perform three specific tasks, the subordinate experiences less uncertainty as to what is to be done. Defining expected behaviors provides the direction and focus needed by many employees, even though it presents a risk of restricting employee creativity and initiative.

Once a manager has identified specific behaviors, the subordinate's later performance can be evaluated in terms of how well the goals were attained. Since the standards are established ahead of time, the manager can be more objective in evaluation.

Finally, and of most importance, a focus on behaviors can minimize defensiveness in an evaluation interaction. Consider the difference between the following statements:

1. "Jim, you really didn't do a very good job on the report."
2. "Jim, the data collection and writing style in the report were fine, but the punctuation was inappropriate in the spots I have indicated."

In our first example, the manager evaluated Jim's performance, but this kind of feedback did not give Jim any ideas as to how to correct his failures. In the second example, Jim was told what behaviors were acceptable. His supervisor identified the sources of difficulty. Description, rather than evaluation, creates a more supportive communication climate. It is important to make the distinction between person and behavior. When a manager has to give negative feedback, resentment is minimized when he can say, "I like you, but I don't like these behaviors."

IDENTIFY THE CRITERIA

A manager can make evaluating employee behavior much easier, and much less subjective, if she defines clear and precise criteria for "comparing" employee performance. The criteria should include all relevent job activities, and they should be weighted as to their relative importance. They give the manager a yardstick with which an employee may be evaluated more objectively. Note the phrasing *more objectively*. Complete objectivity, although desirable, is an unattainable goal, since the manager is always perceiving employee behavior with her own biases, prejudices, blind spots, and unique frames of reference. As additional criteria are used in performance appraisal, such perceptual influences can be reduced.

If criteria for employee behavior are not clearly established, the manager takes the risk of falling into the trap of giving some employees the benefit of the doubt to the point where favoritism emerges. The "halo effect" is a real danger and can create dissension among other employees. If all employees know the criteria and feel that the manager is using those criteria, they will know what to expect. Since doubt and uncertainty have been removed, the employees know what must be done to earn rewards. If the criteria are well established, employees can feel that changing their behaviors and "shaping up" will produce personal benefits. The potential for increased motivation won't appear until the relationship between behaviors and rewards is clearly spelled out and the employees see what it is that the manager is going to reward.

DON'T FOCUS ONLY
ON THE NEGATIVE

It is often difficult to get employees to hear what managers are saying and to appreciate the implications of those messages. All too often employees may sit and listen, but not really hear the intended message. To achieve the desired results, the message must be presented in a way which is, at least minimally, acceptable to the employee. Except for threat, what other strategies are available to the manager to emphasize compatibility when a person is criticized? Criticism in a discipline situation frequently has a negative effect on the achievement of organizational goals and rarely results in an employee changing his problem behavior.

When one is placed in a threatening situation, that person's natural response is to seek protection. If someone throws something at another person, it's only natural for the person to duck and try to avoid the object. The same is true of an employee being criticized. As soon as the inevitable "or else" is heard, the defensiveness begins. One study suggested that defensiveness later results in inferior employee performance.

Managers must communicate to minimize defensiveness. One strategy is to use an indirect approach that sandwiches the negative between positive evaluation and praise. Although some studies have suggested that praise doesn't affect this process one way or another, the research failed to take into account the positioning of bad news in relation to praise. When being criticized, a subordinate's first reaction may well be, "And I suppose I never do anything right." When the manager recognizes and praises the positive behaviors of the subordinate at the beginning of the interview, this counterargument cannot be used. The criticism can be put in perspective and may then be perceived as being more fair.

"Sandwiching" negatives is really just the use of empathy. Putting oneself in another person's place may lead to better predictions on the part of the manager as to how a subordinate may react. The manager may decide in advance to avoid a particular approach. Empathy leads to a look at the employee's particular set of circumstances rather than operating from some neutral stance or from an arbitrary set of rules. Empathy may reduce defensiveness and thus help subordinates hear what is being said.

MINIMIZE THE DIFFERENCES

Minimizing the differences in role status when giving feedback is another way to reduce defensiveness. Instead of telling a subordinate that something is his problem, emphasize a joint concern that must be overcome. This mutual interest allows the subordinate to feel less alone or stuck with the problem. Defensiveness can also be reduced if the evaluated person is not made to feel inferior or second rate. When a manager assumes an arrogant attitude, flaunts his superiority, or just shakes his head in disbelief, a subordinate will invariably become defensive. This is not to suggest that, to prevent a defensive attitude, a manager must renounce his role or have a first-name or buddy relationship with the employee. Instead, the manager must treat subordinates with genuine respect, even though some employee behavior may be unacceptable. A manager must first demonstrate at least a minimal concern for the employee if the employee's work behavior is to be improved materially.

Again, it is obvious that the multiple roles of the manager tend to create conflict. The manager can suggest that although the attainment of organizational goals is a mutual problem, the employee will get no raise because of his poor performance. The manager is to be a counselor, hence the problem is mutual, but the manager must also be an administrator of wages, which, by definition, is a superior role. One way to reduce the conflict is to conduct employee improvement interviews separately from those in which salary matters are discussed. That approach won't eliminate role conflict, but it may help to minimize the negative consequences.

DON'T GUNNYSACK

By giving negative feedback, the manager may want to correct one or two things in the employee's behavior, yet many times the overall objectives get lost once the discussion begins. When the performance confrontation starts to get rough, the participants start digging out all of the ammunition they can muster. All of those little things that have been "under one's skin" finally have a chance to burst out. Everyone has been guilty of that kind of defensive argument, but what are the results of such an approach?

The manager comes into the session with one or two behavioral items to correct. When the employee puts up a fight or gets defensive about some of these things, the manager may feel backed against a wall and strike out with whatever is at hand, such as all those little gripes that have accumulated in the supervisory gunnysack for presenting at the right time. "Gunnysacking" detracts from efforts to correct real problems. The subordinate can now justify his behavior because "obviously the manager is just nitpicking." The message to the employee is diluted if too many additional issues are injected during the discussion. A better strategy is to resolve these minor issues as they arise. If the issues aren't important enough to be brought up as they occur, then they should be forgotten. Gripes must not be allowed to accumulate, lest they create an obstacle when something really important arises.

The effectiveness of feedback often depends on when that feedback is given. When feedback is given immediately following a behavior, the feedback is more likely to be effective. It doesn't make sense to reprimand a child several hours after he has misbehaved. Similarly, it doesn't make sense to withhold evaluative information from an employee until the next six-month evaluation. Feedback, both positive and negative, should be given continuously. Regular feedback allows the subordinates to modify their behavior when necessary, while reinforcing existing desirable behaviors.

THE DIFFERENCE BETWEEN CAN'T AND WON'T

Too often, managers fail to identify the cause of poor performance. Performance has at least two major elements: motivation and ability. If performance is poor, a common managerial response is to assume that the employee won't perform—a motivation problem. Although that may be the case, there are many times when lack of performance is because of the employee's low ability or lack of training. The two factors in poor performance demand very different correction strategies. If the employee won't perform, the manager must evaluate the motivation strategies being used. However, if the employee can't perform, the manager's responsibility is to train the employee, if possible, or to find an alternative solution such as transfer or termination. That important distinction must be made. One way to do so is to directly involve the employee in the performance appraisal process. A joint evaluation procedure not only helps managers to more accurately perceive problems, but it also provides employees with a better understanding of evaluation. It leads to a greater employee satisfaction with the entire evaluation process.

SPLIT THE CONFLICTING ROLES

Some managers have little or no real control over the details of their firm's performance appraisal system. The timing of the supervisor-subordinate joint review session is given, as is the general format of the meeting and the suggested method for presenting bad or negative information. For these managers, the strategy to split conflicting roles will not be possible.

However, for those with a flexible performance review system, a productive approach is to hold two face-to-face sessions with each employee: one dealing with the administration of salaries and rewards or punishments, and a second dealing only with the counseling/planning/training function. Although such an arrangement takes more time—in effect, it can double the actual amount of supervisor-subordinate contact time on each review cycle—the benefits of a split strategy are many. Above all, it permits the supervisor to wear one hat at a time, thus concentrating on a single task without the necessity of shifting from one role to another.

Assuming the first of the two meetings is devoted to the salary/reward phase, the employee has an interim period of time to digest the feedback. Also, if the feedback is negative both the news itself and the employee's offhand reaction are isolated. The counseling phase, or meeting number two, can be held in a more open or productive setting that is relatively uncharged by an emotional response. The employee has the benefit of reflection on the evaluation. With this reflection, the counseling can usually be directed toward more clearly defined and agreed-upon goals. The employee's mind is reasonably clear of evaluative information and is better able to focus on the planning/training session objectives.

Supervisors using a split-session strategy must exercise caution in the second session. Some employees, usually those given low ratings or negative feedback in the first session, will try to resurrect the subject of their rating in the counseling session. It is here that the manager must exert discreet but firm control if the benefits of the split-appraisal approach are to be realized.

WATCH FOR SUPERVISOR DEFENSIVENESS

A new and interesting (although also potentially damaging) phenomenon in performance appraisal is the problem of supervisors perceiving negative employee ratings as reflections on their own abilities. Recently, several supervisors in management seminars conducted by the author have suggested this new barrier to communication in performance appraisal. In such a situation, the supervisor feels that an employee's poor performance directly reflects his own performance as a manager. With that perception, the manager is reluctant to criticize and becomes highly defensive whenever a low-rated employee's defensiveness seems to backfire on the supervisory performance. In some instances, the supervisor's attitude results in the employee's gaining practical control over the performance appraisal process. The minimum cost of such an occurrence is a higher-than-deserved rating. At worst, the entire appraisal process for all employees can be seriously compromised.

There are no simple remedies for such a communication problem. However, should such supervisor defensiveness occur, it may well indicate a performance appraisal failure of another sort at the next higher organizational level. The defensive supervisor's immediate superior has perhaps failed to communicate properly or to conduct meaningful counseling activities with that supervisor. Thus, rater defensiveness may well be a symptom of problems higher up the chain of command.

CONCLUSION

All motivation strategies depend on the efficiency of the evaluation process. Efficiency requires readily understood appraisal procedures and effective managerial communication skills. Despite the incentives used and the objectivity of appraisal mechanisms, evaluation efficiency ultimately depends on the way the manager communicated with the subordinate. It is the responsibility of the manager to be aware of both the pitfalls of the evaluation process and the available communication strategies. Managers facing forthcoming employee performance reviews are advised to consider carefully the ideas and suggestions presented in this chapter. Watch for signs of resentment, gunnysacking, defensiveness, and "fuzzy" criteria. Develop with each employee an acceptable, understandable relationship between the suggestions and standards applicable to the employee and her personal interests. Recognizing and minimizing the differences between the employee's interests and the standards being set is a positive first step toward effective performance appraisal.

FIRING

11
Firing
The Deserving

Firing an employee is a nasty business. The person being fired clearly has a severe problem. Yet, too often, the effect on the company hasn't been considered in terms of a loss of morale in the remaining staff, financial commitments to the departed executive, replacement problems. These things must be considered before, not after, termination of an employee.

The first step in firing an employee is to know exactly why you are doing it. Dipping into the till and chasing secretaries are good reasons, but they're not that common. Three unusual reasons are (1) dead-end job, (2) oversupply, and (3) incompetence. The euphemism for all three is "personality conflict." Breakdown in interpersonal relations is a symptom—not a cause.

"Dead-end" means that a person is receiving pressure from below. Competent subordinates are waiting for promotion, and the person on top has reached her limit. Personality conflicts here show up from below as complaints against promotion policy and against the boss—the one in the dead-end position.

Incompetence means not pleasing the boss. This is the case in which firing comes in stages. First a talk, then a warning, then out. At each stage, there is hope that job performance will change.

TO FIRE
OR NOT TO FIRE

Alternatives to firing aren't hard to find. Transfer, demotion, leave of absence, retraining, and early retirement are all possibilities. When should you consider these courses of action?

Organizations under the gun to cut costs can get away with a harder line, especially in a downward-turning economy, but that's not necessarily to their own best interest. Firms should look carefully before lopping off talent as a fast, effective means of decreasing cash outlay. Some managers get carried away and lose good, irreplaceable people in the name of cost cutting.

Dead-enders may be that way because of bad job-person matching. Oversupply may be temporary. Incompetence may mean that you have not tried to help an employee improve. It is entirely too easy to overlook reductions in travel, postponement of capital expenditures, and other economies and to seize on job terminations as a panacea for rising costs. Thus, it is important to determine that the person being fired for cost-cutting reasons cannot be used in any other capacity.

HARD LINE, SOFT LINE

No alternative? Then the second step is the actual firing. How do you go about it? Two methods are common. Some managers say, "Get the person out—and now." The other side says ease out the employee and help her find another job. Both sides agree that firing shouldn't be disguised or approached obliquely.

Some firing procedures seem designed to make the situation as unpleasant as possible. People are transferred to jobs for which they have no background, are ignored or harassed by their superiors, or are simply passed over again and again.

Tactics designed to freeze out an employee or encourage him to resign only extend the unpleasantness of the situation and damage a department or organization's efficiency and morale. This is called "dehiring," and it can have some bad results. Among the consequences of dehiring are the following:

1. The employee fails to take the hint and quit. The employee may not be very bright, or he may be consciously ignoring the dehiring messages.
2. The employee may feel (with some justification) that the supervisor doesn't have the strength or willingness to fire. The dehiring tactics may thereby undermine the supervisor's authority.
3. The employee may respond to his feeling of the supervisor's weakness by engaging in a sort of "grudge match"—saying, in effect, "Boss, I know you can't fire me, and I'm going to resist all your efforts to get me to leave. I wouldn't leave now even if I wanted to leave!"
4. The employee is aware of the boss's dehiring attempts, but remains in the department as a sort of "wounded bear." In this condition, the employee can do considerable harm to the morale and well-being of other employees.
5. The other employees, aware of the dehiring efforts directed at one of their co-workers, begin to develop sympathy for the problem employee. Even if they were once in favor of the problem person being fired, their reaction to dehiring may be support and defense, and if firing ultimately becomes necessary, it may be far more difficult with fellow employees opposing the decision.

WHAT TO DO WHEN FIRING

Assuming you have chosen to confront rather than prolong, delay, defer, or avoid the problem, the following are some suggestions and strategies for effective firing.

Consult When Making the Decision.   Talk to as many people as necessary to reduce your own uncertainty and to be sure that the decision, once made, is irrevocable. This does not mean that the employee's job performance or present status should be known throughout the organization. Consultations should be done privately, at a high enough level to insure confidentiality.

If you do consult with your peers, be sure they know the importance of remaining silent. One of the worst things that can occur when firing is for the employee to learn of what is about to happen through the grapevine.

Make Sure There Is No Alternative.   Under no circumstances should an employee be kept on the payroll simply as a reward for seniority, loyalty, or as a balm to the company's conscience. The problem certainly will not be remedied by transferring the person to a responsibility beneath her actual or imagined capabilities, for that would only aggravate the situation. Consider first the twin responsibilities of the dignity of the terminated employee and the best interests of the company.

Do Not Prolong Termination.   In most cases, it is wiser to determine a fair severance arrangement and to terminate the person immediately. It is rarely wise to retain the employee on the payroll until he relocates. The person's interests and energies will obviously be directed toward job hunting—not to his job duties. This was the position of Admiral Stansfield Turner in his well-publicized reduction in the work force of the CIA. Early in 1978, Admiral Turner swiftly and effectively fired a large number of employees. Despite the initial shock, such an action is far better for employee and agency alike than the more "humane" approach of a slow firing. Slow firing is about as humane as snipping off a dog's tail one inch at a time!

Plan to Tell the Employee at the End of the Day and Week.   Telling a person he is fired and then leaving that employee to continue working as though nothing has happened is cruel and unrealistic. The employee is not going to do much work, and he may be resentful enough to want to create trouble. If there is support for the problem employee, other employees may consider some sort of work action, such as a slowdown or wildcat strike. If the other employees know someone has been fired, they may make things uncomfortable for the leaving employee.

For all these reasons, it's best to fire at the end of the day or the end of the workshift, and late in the week.

Do It Where You Are Comfortable and in Control.   Physical setting is just as important when firing as it is when counseling or disciplining an employee. But there are some important differences. In counseling, you want to minimize the status differences, trying to encourage the employee to make a commitment to change. When firing, it is best for the employee if a supervisor consciously uses the symbols and tools of the supervisory position.

Sit behind a desk, directly across from the employee. Keep both hands folded on the desk in front of you, and have all your other materials available, but not directly in front of you. Keep the lighting even and avoid glare either in the employee's direction or your own.

Have All the Facts.   When talking to the employee, have all the relevant facts available. If the employee wants to hear those facts, be as direct as possible. At minimum, have the employee's personnel file with you, supplemented by whatever additional information is appropriate.

Be Direct, Clear, and Honest.   Tell the person candidly and forthrightly that he is being terminated and exactly why. Be blunt, but not brutal. Maintain eye contact.

Try to avoid such euphemisms as "we can't use you anymore," "you'll have to go," "hope you can find meaningful work in another organization," or "we're letting you go." Call the action what it is—fired, terminated. Fuzzy language may seem more humane, but it may result in the employee dangling with false hope.

A fine dramatic example of this false hope occurred on the last episode of the "Mary Tyler Moore Show" on CBS-TV (1978). Mary and her male co-workers were summoned to the office of their new boss, who announced, "Ted, you stay—the rest of you guys are fired!" All returned to their offices, and Mary started to think, Hey, he said "guys." I'm not a guy, so he didn't mean *me!* She called the boss with this flicker of hope, only to be told again, this time more clearly, that she too had been fired. A poignant moment, all too real when employees don't understand what has happened to them.

Take the Heat Yourself.   It may be convenient and more comfortable for a supervisor to pass the blame for a firing decision to a faceless group usually known as "them." Such statements as "it has been decided" and "they (higher management) have concluded" help take the heat off the supervisor, who can appear almost as a passive, disinterested observer rather than as the "culprit" who actually made the decision. Some firing decisions *are* made by higher-ups. The supervisor may be merely a conduit and may actually disagree with the decision to fire, but except in these cases, it is best for the supervisor to state directly, "I have decided to terminate your contract with this firm." The employee has a target for wrath, but is much less likely to be frustrated with this message than with the vague, faceless "them." It is frustration from an inability to get hold of responsibility that leads to most post-firing difficulties. Reducing that frustration with a direct statement is best.

Don't Apologize—or Give Hope.   Once the message "you're fired" has been delivered, there's a temptation to soften the blow with an apology. To the supervisor, "I'm sorry" may mean "I regret the position you're in." To the employee, it may mean "I'd do something to change things if I could."

Express concern and genuine personal regret in nonverbal ways. Give the employee a chance to blow off steam without interruption, and don't be patronizing with such statements as, "someday you'll find this was all for the best."

Don't communicate anything to the individual that in any way makes the firing decision seem tentative or subject to appeal. If the person asks if there is any appeal or chance for a change in the decision, simply reply no.

Consider Having a Witness.   In most firings, a witness is unnecessary. The two individuals can communicate without the need for verification. If there is any chance that hostility will turn into physical threat, or if there is a chance for legal action by the employee, a witness is a good protection. Some organizations require that a witness be present in all firing meetings.

The witness should be standing or seated where she can see and hear everything that happens, but she should not be too conspicuous. Introducing the witness is optional. Don't stand or sit next to the witness in a way that suggests an inquisition or tribunal facing the employee. Such an arrangement can create considerable defensiveness.

Have All Contractual Materials with You.   Most organizations have forms and documents to account for keys, badges, passes, equipment, and other things used by an employee. Referring to these materials and working with the employee to recover them can divert attention from the actual firing message. It gives supervisor and employee something to talk about. Keep in mind that most in-processing done with new employees must now be undone.

At this time, tell the employee the details about company cars, transferring insurance protection, pension benefits information, and the last paycheck. This is useful information. It can answer some of the many questions that are bound to occur to the employee, and it can help overcome the awkward silence after the message has been delivered.

Be sure to hold off discussing these details until you are sure the employee is through blowing off steam. Cutting off this emotional outlet too early can have damaging consequences.

Make a Record of All That Is Said.   Take notes, or use a tape recorder. In some firms, a transcript of the entire meeting is signed by both supervisor and employee, attesting to its accurracy. Take careful note of threats, innuendoes, and accusations, and be mindful of what things may have been left unsaid or undone.

Provide What Help You Can.   Write fair letters of recommendation. Offer the services of the company psychologist for counseling, if appropriate. Make sure that the person carries away with him the same version of the termination as the company's in order to avoid difficulties in reference checking.

Inform the Other Employees.   As we have discussed, the grapevine is always at work, especially on such emotional matters as firings. Plan to announce the firing decision to the fired employee's co-workers as soon as possible. Make your announcement *only* when the fired employee is not present.

Tell them directly, "Ed has been terminated." Respond to questions carefully, and be mindful of libel possibilities if you say too much or if you treat as fact something that is only an inference. The other employees are looking for reassurance, not details. Reassurance is much safer, since it focuses on what the other employees need rather than on the shortcomings of the fired worker.

There is always a possibility that the fired worker has already told fellow employees about the firing, with his version of what happened. Assuming that the fired employee is not present, avoid an argument with other employees over the interpretation of details. Such a discussion serves no useful purpose and may trap you into saying something you should not say.

Maintain Friendship.   It is to your advantage. Poor handling of an employee termination can tarnish a company's reputation, along with the reputation of the manager who actually does the firing.

Hard-line firing or soft-line ease-out—either way, there may be repercussions. First, there is the loss of investment in the person who has left. Training time and money are lost. Many companies are paying the costs of relocating certain executives who have been dropped because of merger or acquisition. Many companies are preserving their reputations by trying to be as nice as possible when an executive just can't be kept, even though the story is just an excuse for firing when poor performance is the real reason. These companies (and their managers) are not going to fare well in the eyes of those who had to go.

However, there are other, less apparent costs. An employee who has had a relatively short tenure has not paid off her recruitment and relocation expense to the company. The cost of hiring a replacement will probably be higher than it was to hire the person who was fired. One bright spot (maybe) is that the company that picks up the fired employee will probably put out more money to get her than it cost your company to fire her.

If firing is absolutely necessary, an analytical approach to the problem is best. Analyze your attitudes toward this investment in human talent with as much vigor as you would approach capital investments.

Morale is rarely a cost item when a firing is clearly deserved; however, there can be some horrible examples. For instance, one company was trapped by circumstances, and morale did suffer badly. An executive with a lot of seniority, a good reputation, and a good work record was suddenly found to be a drug addict. He was fired immediately, but, to protect his and the company's reputation, no one was told the exact reason. Needless to say, it looked like a good man was bounced arbitrarily. Fortunately, that kind of incident is rare.

The real cost of firing is to the concept of management continuity. Management continuity is a basic and important function of all organizations. Accordingly, prior to any decision on employee firing, you should conduct a careful and thoughtful analysis of your management "talent" depth. Is the decision to eliminate the person absolutely necessary? Is the decision being reached in panic? With an upturn in business, would the terminated person's talents be sorely missed? Employee firing must be considered in terms of its long-range impact on your department's growth.

SCARS

For many, firing is the ultimate rejection. There are six important consequences for the fired employee.

1. Loss of income. Financial security is threatened. Living habits have to change.
2. Change in the routine. No job means no commuting, no lunch with friends, no need to get up on time in the morning. Total disruption.
3. Family tension. Spouses get upset during job hunting. Family quarrels that develop can result in scars that take a long time to heal.
4. "Masculinity" crisis for men. The feeling that the manly role is not being fulfilled. Sexual problems among the fired are frequent.
5. Public humiliation. There is a feeling of being held up as a loser before the eyes of friends, relatives, and the public at large.
6. Job hunting. Searching for another job can be a demoralizing proposition. Rejection seems to follow rejection, making it harder to keep up the pace.

RESIGN OR BE FIRED?

One final thought on firing versus the alternatives: Some managers feel that employees on the brink of being fired should be allowed to offer their resignation instead.

In favor of this approach is the opportunity to reduce some of the negative feelings the former employee may have about the organization. A resignation makes it possible for the individual to maintain a public self-image and may make it easier for her to get another job. A resignation also gives the manager a chance to offer the employee a choice instead of a *fait accompli*.

On the negative side, if you tell an employee that she will be fired if she does not resign and the employee chooses to resign, the firm may later find that the action was considered a layoff. The employee would be entitled to unemployment compensation.

CONCLUSION

Firing is never pleasant, and it rarely leaves us with the feeling that we have done our best. Yet willingness to go to the limit is one of the prime requisites for managerial success.

Fire with care, and only after thoughtful review. Explore other less costly alternatives, but keep in mind that for many problem employees, firing may become the only solution available.

It is for managers the ultimate organizational weapon. Like any "ultimate weapon," it should be handled with respect—and a willingness to use it if necessary.

12
Firing
The Undeserving

Y ou're fired!"

Those words carry a cruel ring for almost anyone. They convey a sense of "unwantedness," a blow to the ego, not to mention the pocketbook. To the employee who is fired because of his personal actions or general behavior, there is a possibility that the punishment fits the crime. Those deservedly fired may not agree they are deserving, but at least they can point to an event or events and thus develop some sort of personal explanation.

But what about the person whose actions or behavior did not directly bring about a termination? For this man or woman, firing will seem (and may in reality be) more brutal, more unfair, more outrageous than it might be for those who deserve to be fired.

Still, people are "undeservedly" fired for a number of reasons. Some companies and organizations prefer to label their actions "strategic terminations," "outplacement," "terminal layoff," "reduction in forces," "dehiring," even "termination without prejudice." No matter what it is called, the result is the same: A previously valued employee, apparently doing a good job, is now involuntarily unemployed.

WHY FIRE THOSE WHO DON'T DESERVE IT?

There are as many reasons for firing as there are labels. Some of the more common (and practical) reasons are as follows:

1. Drop in business, requiring fewer managers or employees.
2. Going out of business. This is the extreme case, since technically everyone is fired.
3. Consolidations. One organization buys out or takes over another, and duplicate staffs are unnecessary.
4. Reorganization. Same as 3, only internally.
5. Technology changes. Usually bringing with the change a built-in obsolescence for the practitioners of the old technology who didn't (or couldn't) keep up.
6. Cuts in funding for a division, section, department, or group.
7. Change in top administration or at other levels below the top.
8. A person better qualified for a position becomes available, making the incumbent unnecessary.
9. The boss's son (daughter, in-law, mother, etc.) needs a position. Same as 8 above, although "better qualified" may be questionable.
10. Mandatory retirement. Becoming passé, but still a factor in some situations.

The common factor in all of these reasons (with the possible exception of 5) is that the person or persons being fired did not directly create the conditions that brought about the need to fire. It can be argued that in some cases a person's general failure (especially at the top administrative or managerial levels) may have contributed to the firm's loss of market position, sales, occupancy, etc.; still, for most managerial people, the reasons cited for "undeserved firing" will leave them with the feeling that they have been wronged.

WHY WORRY ABOUT SUCH FIRINGS?

No one has an absolute, no-cut lock on a job forever. Some star athletes, tenured college professors, and the boss's relatives seem to be better protected than most people, but they suffer their share of undeserved firings, too. When business gets really tough, the boss may begin to weigh domestic peace and harmony with the dollar cost of retaining brother-in-law LeRoy. It can happen anywhere, to anyone. Applying the golden rule, one answer to "so what?" is, "I'd like humane treatment and help relocating if I got fired, so I'd better be prepared to give humane treatment when necessary."

On another level, proper treatment of those fired undeservedly is a powerful message to those who remain with the organization. Assuming there will be someone left when the firing is over, their output, commitment, and loyalty is essential. If those remaining, already sensitive to the undeserving nature of the firing, sense that their former fellow employee was shabbily treated, their behavior is likely to suffer.

A third reason for delicacy, concern, and genuine help for those undeservedly fired is commitment. The person fired doubtless had a commitment to the organization, a commitment that showed in his work, his off-the-job statements about the organization, and the personal/professional relationship he maintained with the boss. All of this suggests a reciprocal commitment from the organization and its management to provide transition support.

A company's community image and standing must also be considered. Some persons will turn what they consider an unjustified firing or layoff into a cause célèbre. They will be able to generate media interest and public sympathy for their position. Most organizations have at least a passing concern for public opinion and public good will, and many organizations have a definite need for public acceptance and support. Thus, a generally positive public reaction to a firing is very important—if there is to be any public reaction at all. Heading off a fired employee's desire to "go public" is a prime consideration in effectively handling these situations.

Beyond a general public reaction to an undeserved firing, managers should be concerned about more specific public responses. For example, a fired accountant will have contacts in the accounting community. These contacts, if they are given a story of unfairness or shabby treatment of a colleague, may have an impact on future hiring retention of other professionally related individuals, as well as on the behavior and attitudes of those persons whose cooperation a company needs.

Finally, a major reason for effectively and humanely firing the undeserving is simple decency. The individual is blameless, largely a victim of circumstances. Understanding, compassion, and realistic help and counsel are *owed* to the person being fired.

HOW SHOULD THE FIRING BE HANDLED?

As in firing those who deserve to be fired, there is no foolproof way to deliver the message to the undeserving. Some of the same concerns and techniques apply in both situations, but for some of the reasons we have discussed above, the undeserved firing should be handled a little differently. Following are some techniques and considerations:

Adopt a "You" Viewpoint—but Don't Overdo.   In Chapter 4, we discussed the value of a "you" viewpoint. It involves looking at a problem and framing a message from the receiver's point of view. In doing so, we help the receiver understand the message and thereby respond positively to it.

Although a "you" viewpoint is useful, it can be overdone, especially in an undeserved firing. Trying to show the newly unemployed how the action will result in new challenges, new career opportunities, more leisure, and more freedom may actually be perceived as condescension, or as rubbing salt in the wounds. Avoid saying "I know how you feel" or "I can sympathize with you." You can't know how she really feels unless you've been there before. Even if you have, there will be a big credibility gap between you and the fired—a gap that's almost impossible to bridge with simple statements. A useful "you view" approach is to be willing to listen and to provide nonverbal support. Ask "would you care to talk about it?" if there is an apparent desire to do so. Then listen attentively, nodding and keeping close, empathetic eye contact. Don't attempt to justify or defend if the other person begins placing blame—although you want to be careful not to agree with him when there is an obvious attempt to brand the company with wrongdoing. While listening, attempt to focus on the positive, but do it sparingly, and only if you feel it will be taken in a positive way. Don't overpaint a too-glossy picture. After all, it is still an undeserved firing in the mind of the other person.

Don't Offer Excuses.   There are any number of excuses (we might prefer to call them reasons) why the undeserving employee is being fired. The decision to fire was doubtless made after careful thought and analysis. The reasons may be complex, and those reasons led to the unavoidable conclusion that is now facing the employee. Despite the logic and the inescapable validity of these reasons, they offer cold comfort to the fired. In Chapter 10, we suggested that bad news be sandwiched between items of good news. The purpose of this sandwich is to put the receiver of the bad news into a receptive mood. Of course, in performance appraisal, we are trying to change a person's behavior, and we use the positive parts of the message to accomplish the change. In firing the undeserving, the positive outcome of the firing may only heighten the dismay the employee feels. For example; "Once this staff cutback is complete, the company will be in a far better competitive position. We'll be able to hold down our prices and build up the business. We'll be in much better shape than we're in today." Wonderful.

As an ex-employee, how would you feel? The difference between a reason and an excuse is in the eye of the beholder.

An excuse is much like an apology—it may beg the question: "If you're *that* sorry, or if there's *that much* of a reason, why me?"

Although reasons—or excuses—should not be volunteered, they should be prepared for those who want reasons. Some fired persons want reassurance that the actions taken were not in any way related to their past performance.

Avoid Blame.   Reassure the fired person that her past performance is not the reason for the firing, but don't overdo this reassurance, since painting a too glowing picture of the employee's worth may make the firing seem all the more undeserved. Have the complete reason for firing this specific employee, but keep the focus on a discussion of the real reasons for *all* of the firings. Show the employee all of the conditions that made firing necessary. Avoid any discussion of "why me, and not Al?" This question forces a comparison between two employees and only reinforces the "unfairness" of the decision reached. If you answer the question honestly, you may reveal factors that were relevant to the decision but irritating to the fired. For example,

> "If we fired Al, we would lose valuable experience."
> "After all, Al is black, and although your record and his are the same, we have to keep him because of our affirmative action commitments."
> "On balance, Al has fewer negatives for us than you."

All of these responses may be honest and realistic, but any one of them would only inflame an already irritated person.

Another approach to the "me or Al" question is lying. This is dangerous. It is no more likely to soothe the employee than is honesty. It may also bring into the conversation factors that can create future problems.

Have All the Facts; Use Only What You Need.   Have all the information that relates to the general conditions surrounding the firing and to the individual's specific situation. Also, the person delivering the fire message should have all the employee's records. This makes it possible to answer specific questions about continuation of hospitalization, life and accident insurance, return of company vehicles, profit sharing and company stock ownership plans, and similar details.

In suggesting that the person doing the firing use only the information needed, we refer to the details surrounding the decision to fire. As noted above, the employee should be given as much information as possible about the reasons for the action taken, as long as those reasons do not suggest that he was personally responsible for bringing about this decision. To suggest personal blame is to risk recriminations, uncomfortable confrontations, and possible "wrongful dismissal" lawsuits. Still, having all the facts can make the firer more comfortable and can at least give the fired individual the feeling that this action, however distasteful, was thought through before action was taken.

Separate the Action from the Reason.   Make clear to the fired person that this action in no way reflects his personal worth. Keep out of your conversation any mention of past errors, problems, or difficulties. Even though such past actions were in no way related to the firing, mention of them now may cause the fired person to assume that the firing was for this past sin. Keep in mind that firing is a disconfirming message, one very likely to be taken personally. Emphasize and reemphasize that the firing was not the person's doing in any way.

Offer Recommendations.   One way to show the company's good will—and to create some good will with the fired person—is to offer letters of recommendation. Many managers have found that having "to whom it may concern" letters of recommendation at the firing meeting is a good approach. The fired person has something tangible to take away, along with an indication of the kinds of specifically addressed recommendations he will be able to get later from the company. This is better than merely promising a recommendation. It can be an important source of reassurance.

Offer Real Assistance.   Beyond recommendations, offer the fired employee real assistance in either finding other employment or in making the transition to retirement. Some areas for assistance include the following:

1. Help in preparing, typing, or printing resumes.
2. Counseling on taking job interviews.
3. Job search counseling; how to look for a job.
4. Placement services. Many firms operate outplacement for their undeserving fired; others use established employment agencies or executive search firms; some even go so far as to pay the fees connected with an ex-employee's job search.
5. Personal—or family—counseling. This can be helpful in relieving some of the fired person's anxiety and can help remove or alleviate an important burden—the family's reaction to the firing.
6. Transitional office and secretarial facilities—preferably away from the company's main offices or facilities. Putting temporary offices near the person's old office location increases the chance of the person running into former colleagues, which can be very uncomfortable.
7. Home sale/relocation help.
8. Financial help. Severance and accrued vacation pay, continuation of hospitalization coverage and insurance during a transition period, low interest short-term loans.

Many of these helps are covered by company policies and may be beyond any individual manager's ability to grant. If such transitional help is not available, or is prohibited, changes in policy should be started. The golden rule applies here. We never know when we might be on the receiving end of the help for the undeservedly fired.

Do It Soon.   Once a decision to cut the work force has been made, do the firing quickly. Don't let the company grapevine create unnecessary pain for those being fired. Remember that no organization is immune to leaks, especially when something as important as lost jobs is concerned. The entertainment press is full of stories about how television people come to work one day to find the set to their series locked, the series canceled. Or a headline announces a widespread reduction-in-force, naming those divisions and departments being cut. Aside from the impact such leaks have on those leaving, consider the effect on those staying.

Fire Everyone at Once.   If many people are to be fired, tell them—one by one—at the same time. If this isn't done, a "deathwatch" results, which can destroy morale and make subsequent firings emotionally more difficult. In *Ball Four*,[1] author Jim Bouton tells of baseball players conducting a deathwatch every time a player is called unexpectedly into the manager's office. Some of this behavior cannot be avoided. Too much of it can destroy a firm's ability to regroup and pull together after a number of undeserved firings.

Be Prepared for Backlash.   It is impossible to predict how a person is apt to respond to a "you're fired" message—especially when it is undeserved or a complete surprise. Realize the stress the person is under, and be prepared for any contingency. Some people cry, others shout or threaten, still others just stare blankly into space. Allow time and room for emotional responses, as long as they are within reasonable control and pose no personal threat to the person doing the firing.

Be prepared for a delayed reaction to the firing. Often hearing that a person fired some time ago has committed suicide or taken up drinking or drugs to excess can have a profound impact on the person who did the firing. If you have followed all the proper, humane, and reasonable steps in firing the undeserving, there is no need to feel either guilt or a sense of debt. Be mindful of the negative psychological effects of firing on the firer.

Use Space Wisely.   Arrange the setting for the firing so that the person being fired is not directly across from the person delivering the message. Get both persons at a desk or a table on adjacent sides. Use subdued lighting, and avoid glare from exposed bulbs or undraped windows. If there is music piped into the office, turn it off. Permit no interruption for any reason. If possible, use an office that has a second exit, so that the person fired can leave without having to immediately face people in a reception area or entrance hallway. Use much more care in choosing and arranging the spaces for firing the undeserving than is necessary for those being fired because of their own actions.

Permit Face Saving.   A major blow from any firing, especially one that is undeserved, is the reaction from friends, family, and co-workers. Even if the person fired is blameless and others are being fired too, there is still a need to save face. Efforts should go beyond providing a separate exit.

If possible (in keeping with company policy) permit the fired the choice of resigning without affecting his or her termination benefits. By being able to say "I quit," the fired person may feel less of a blow to pride and self-esteem. This will not be so important when large numbers of persons are being fired together. It can be very important when only one or two persons are being fired undeservingly.

Payoff for No Work.   Consider a policy of paying a person's regular salary from the time of firing until formally separating. If a person who is fired—deservingly or undeservingly—remains on the job for a few more days or weeks, little productive work will result. Further, the fired person may "poison the well," lowering the morale and productivity of those who remain.

Have a Media Stategy.   Most persons fired with or without personal blame go quietly. Few want to bring any further attention to themselves or their plight. They simply want to blend in and start working again as soon as possible.

There are exceptions. Be prepared for that isolated person who takes his case to the local media. Although there is little chance that media exposure of an undeserved firing will harm a company, bad publicity never does any good. Most firms try to avoid such notice and to minimize any damage from media coverage.

Consult legal counsel about your response to media questions. In general, the rules for handling media inquiries are simple:

1. Say as little as possible.
2. Give no specific details about the individual who is being fired.
3. Answer *only* general questions.
4. Do not engage in a debate with the fired employee with media people present.
5. Do not become identified as a "company representative"—it could be harmful to your future career.
6. Have counsel present *every time* there is a media contact.

Beyond these tips, have a general media strategy in mind as a part of the plan to fire certain people. Having a plan, even in rough outline form, can help avoid a poor reaction that can harm everyone involved.

Do Not Admit Legal Implications.   Today there is a dramatic rise in "wrongful dismissal" suits filed by fired employees. Some of these suits have a basis in law; most do not. Every such lawsuit, well founded or not, is costly in terms of time, money, effort, publicity, and lost good will. Although there is nothing to prevent a fired employee from filing a wrongful dismissal, don't encourage one with an offhanded remark such as "you just might have a case." You may start the fired employee thinking "lawsuit." Know the possible legal ramifications of each firing, and don't look for trouble.

Be Sure the Union Knows.   When fired employees are represented by a labor union, be sure the union has been informed about management's actions, the full scope of those actions, and the reasons for those actions—before they occur. This may seem obvious, but a surprising number of firms and managers who fail to do so quickly find themselves in big trouble that is often unnecessary.

Avoid Any Appearance of "Dehiring".   As we have discussed, dehiring is a strategy of encouraging a person to voluntarily resign rather than being fired outright. When dealing with those who do not deserve to be fired, there are apt to be some dehiring efforts at work. After all, every prospective person to be fired who quits first is one less problem to confront. But as we have seen, dehiring often does not work, and it can leave scars on both those fired and those employees who remain. As much as possible before actually delivering the "you're fired" message, avoid telegraphing or leaking the message through inadvertent slights or slurs. Avoid overreaction—which may border on hypocrisy—but don't dehire. Those being fired through no fault of their own deserve better.

Avoid Creating False Hopes.   When firing the undeserving, it is wise to maintain as much of an optimistic attitude as possible. If there is a real chance that the fired person can be rehired in the near future, say so—cautiously. Don't give a specific timetable, and don't suggest rehiring unless you have a high degree of certainty that it will happen. Because of the negative feelings that exist in a firing interview, many managers try to reduce the tension by holding out hope that's really not there. When they do, they only add to the fired person's sense of disappointment and disillusion. Use the possibility of rehiring cautiously, and only when it is justified.

Consider the Impact on Those Staying.   The impact on those staying is an important issue, one we have touched on several times. Whenever there is any change in the composition of a work group, the group members want to know what is going on, how the change affects them personally, and what changes—if any—are coming next. This is true when new people are hired for a group, when people are reassigned, when they voluntarily leave, or when they are fired for cause. Concern, anxiety, even paranoia are usually at a peak when one or more persons in a group are fired undeservedly. The same feelings develop among all employees when an entire group or department is fired. Assuming the decision to fire was made for sound reasons, it is important to consider the impact of the firing on those who remain. Provide them with continuous communication. This does not necessarily mean telling them all the details of the firing, especially since those fired have a right to privacy, but it does mean providing reassurance, emotional support, and as much of a sense of well-being as possible. Provide open-discussion times when employees' questions and anxieties can be aired, and be willing to frankly discuss the situation as it unfold and develops. Point out the benefits of a streamlined, more efficient organization, and be sure these benefits are communicated in terms that appeal to the employees' needs instead of the company's.

Under no circumstances, make any unkind or derogatory comments about the person or persons fired. Doing so can result in a direct blow to morale.

Don't (Let Someone Else Do It).   It might seem that the coward's way out of the dilemma of having to fire someone who doesn't deserve to be fired is to avoid the whole uncomfortable mess and bring in someone else to do the nasty deed.

It may seem callous, but there are some sound reasons for doing so. For example, if the person being fired is likely to become violent, it might be safer to have a person capable of handling violence deliver this message. Or, where there is a possibility of threats being carried out against the firer, an anonymous out-of-towner may help avoid further trouble. One manager, faced with a decision to fire an employee, had the following conversation during a confrontation that was supposed to be the termination interview. We can assume that the employee knew what was coming.

MANAGER: "John, as you know, the company is having to make some tough decisions about its employees."
EMPLOYEE: "Do you like guns?"
MANAGER: "Why—no, I'm not really into guns."
EMPLOYEE: "I collect guns—would you like to see my guns?"
MANAGER: "Uh, John, perhaps some other time—since you're one of the employees who will be staying on with the company, we're expecting . . ."

Was this a veiled threat? The manager thought so and backed down from his decision. Later, when it became obvious that John would have to go, an outside came in to handle the termination interview.

In some situations, there is a need for wholesale firings, and management fears that there will be considerable resentment of management from those who remain. An outsider (or group of outsiders) can do the deed and help the company maintain some greater measure of employee good will. Here's an example:

Company X was faced with serious changes in its competitive environment. In the opinion of top management, the ranks of middle management were overgrown with people whose skills and abilities were obsolete. There was a need to immediately discharge 40 percent of their middle management.

The problem was the devastating effect such a firing would have on those who remained with the company. Many of the employees had been with the company for years, and they believed they had lifetime jobs.

The solution was to bring in an outsider. He was introduced to the employees and managers as a replacement for one of the managers who recently received a promotion. Only a few people at the top of the organization knew the real mission of this outsider. His job over the next year was to thoroughly analyze the company's operation, recommend which persons should be fired, and then follow through with the actual firings. Before starting on his new job, this individual had a firm understanding with those who hired him that:

1. He would recommend whom to fire, but the top-level management would make the final decision.
2. The actual fire messages were his to deliver.
3. At the end of the year, the outsider would be publicly "fired" by top management—for the reason that he had gone too far in bringing about change in the company.

If this sounds a bit too staged, you're right. Both the outsider's job and his firing were predetermined. When his job was finished, and his own firing was announced, top management was able to shift most of the public blame for the mass firings to this scapegoat. Top management could also bring in another manager to take over the smaller, leaner organization, and that manager would be free of the emotional baggage that would accompany anyone who had just fired 40 percent of the work force.

If both of these examples seem unrealistic, or rarely likely to happen, consider that in most organizations managers go out of their way to avoid having to deliver firing messages, even to those who deserve to be fired. This invariably leads to the firing message being delivered either in a hinting way (dehiring) or by an unknown third party. Either way, there are some serious negative consequences of a passive strategy of letting someone else fire the undeserving employee.

COMPANY POLICY

In several strategies and considerations above, we referred to company policy. A well-designed and well-implemented company policy that covers firing the undeserved can be a big help in avoiding charges of unequal or insensitive treatment. It can also help managers who face the prospect of firing employees for reasons that are not of their doing.

Reviewing the "undeserved firing" policies and practices of many companies, we have found many common characteristics. Following are some of the better ones:

1. *Recommendations* offered in either a "to whom it may concern" format or specifically addressed to a prospective employer. Some firms have found good results permitting their ex-employees review privileges. This way, employees can see for themselves the recommendations they are getting. In the process, they also see the company's commitment to helping them find work.

2. *Outplacement,* running the gamut from help with resumes and interviews through active placement services either provided by the firing firm or prepaid with an outside professional firm.

3. *Resume writing help.* A brief summary of resume-writing considerations is in the Appendix of this book.

4. *Loans.* Short-term low interest (or below market) loans can help a fired person relocate into business or live comfortably while looking for another job. Offering such a loan helps maintain the good will of the former employee. This can be especially important if the ex-employee finds work with a competing firm and trade secrets are involved. Some companies even build trade-secret security provisions into loan agreements, if they do not otherwise exist in an employee's contract.

5. *Transition benefits* permitting an employee to continue hospitalization, group insurance, stock purchase plans, and use of a company car for a specified time period. All such benefits cease as soon as the employee starts work for another firm.

6. *Counseling.* Group or individual therapy to help the in-

dividual deal with the emotional and psychological problems of being fired. This is especially valuable for older employees. Even though they may have some pension protection, unexpected firing in this way can result in severe depression and other psychological reaction. Company-paid individual therapy is also on the increase, as is psychological help for spouses and families of those undeservedly fired.

7. *Transition aid.* Use of a company-paid office, secretarial and typing help, and copying and computer-processing time can help an individual make the transition to unemployment. It can also be a big help in the person's job search. As we noted earlier, such transition facilities should be separate from the firm's main offices and facilities.

8. *Consultancy.* For those who have a useful skill or experience that could be used elsewhere in the company, a short-term consultancy can be a useful way to bridge the employment gap—both financially and psychologically. Consultancies of this sort should be short-term and preferably should keep the individual from direct frequent contact with her former colleagues and co-workers. If a consultancy is offered, be sure the person taking it knows *all the terms* of the contract. Make it clear that the consultancy is neither a substitute for regular employment nor a bridge to future rehiring. Also make clear what benefits and prerequisites go with the consultancy—especially since they are likely to differ markedly from those that go with regular employment.

9. *Termination contracts,* in contractual form, spell out all details of the separation. In addition to those areas discussed above, spell out stock buy-back provisions, severance compensation, and requirements and responsibilities relating to company secrets, patents, etc. Such a contract helps to reduce the fired employee's uncertainty and can measurably reduce the incidence of wrongful dismissal suits later.

10. *Employment contracts.* Many firms are now detailing "undeserved firing" terms in their standard employment contracts offered to managerial, technical, and professional personnel. Such an approach is the ultimate in "proactive" or anticipatory management. It can pay off in many ways.

CONCLUSION

In this chapter, we have used the term "undeserved firing" to cover every situation where a person's employment is terminated for reasons other than those related directly to his or her performance. Such firing is perhaps the most difficult responsibility any manager faces. Done properly, with concern for the person being fired and for those who remain, it can be an important (if reluctantly used) option in any manager's arsenal. We have painted undeserved firing as the most difficult managerial chore, the one used as an absolute last resort. It should be, but there are times when it must be used. Do it cautiously, carefully, humanely, and intelligently.

13
The Legal Considerations In Firing

In previous chapters, we discussed the managerial and communication issues relating to firing. In this chapter, we will look at the legal issues. Certain laws covering termination are part of the "legal bedrock" of personnel. Other laws, presidential orders, and court and administrative law decisions are new. Their real impact and effect is not yet known. Interpretation of statutes varies from one legal jurisdiction to another. New laws, orders, rules, and court decisions appear every day. There are few constants in the law as it relates to firing.

Some managers experienced in firing matters suggest that the only sure thing in firing today is the growth in the number of wrongful dismissal suits. We have become the lawsuit society, going to court for relief over an amazing array of issues.

This chapter deals with the legal basics of firing. It is as up-to-date as possible, but before relying on our advice, consult legal counsel. Use the following information as a guide. Plan before problems arise to avoid the obvious legal difficulties, and seek professional help whenever there is any doubt about your legal position or that of your organization.

LEGALLY ACCEPTABLE
REASONS FOR DISMISSAL

Reasons for dismissal can include the following: continuous illness, incompetence, neglect of duty, negligence, intoxication, disobedience of company rules (e.g., not wearing a safety hat, goggles), insolence, and disrespect. Many cases evolve because of misunderstandings between employee and employer—especially in the commissions area. The employer believes he has made clear how commissions are determined, and the employee interprets it as something entirely different. Therefore, it is extremely important to carefully document—but document everyone—each person violating a rule, etc.

For nonunion or no-contract employees, the employer can summarily fire an employee. For union or contract employees, the contract will state reasons for which an employee can be fired. If a contract is for one year, it can simply not be renewed. Unions are especially sensitive in matters affecting anything negotiated by contract or seniority (people with less seniority are fired first). However, never fire or discipline an employee because of his union activity. Any serious disciplinary action during a union organizing campaign, particularly a discharge, involving a worker who has supported the union will almost automatically result in the filing of an unfair labor practice charge with the National Labor Relations Board (NLRB) claiming that the employee was discharged because of his union activity.

Termination of employment for sickness or unauthorized holiday leave must be justified to the satisfaction of the courts should the employee file suit. Dismissal for acts of dishonesty require extremely well-thought-out, planned legal strategy. Before any decision is made, there must be a thorough investigation. Reasons coming to light after the dismissal (and during the appeal process) cannot be used to justify the dismissal. Proof of guilt is not required: What is needed are reasonable grounds for inferring or suspecting dishonesty.

Managers with experience as supervisors in union-oriented companies stress the importance of *documentation*. More important, however, is the extent of fairness and evenness that management shows in documentation. For example, if a certain employee is documented for tardiness, it is important that *all* tardy employees be so documented. You may single out a problem, but you may not single out an employee.

And just because an employee has been doing something against company rules or policy for some time you cannot necessarily dismiss him. This is the case even if it has been documented. If an employee has been consistently late returning from breaks, the manager must notify *all* employees that "in the future, employees arriving late from breaks will be violating company rules, and management will from now on enforce the rules!" One employee cannot be dismissed for coming in late or coming back late from a break if other employees are also coming in late.

WHO CAN FIRE?

In general, any employer has the right to fire, even without a reason, as long as it does not fall within the range of discrimination or violate the law. (Discrimination comes under Title VII of the Civil Rights Act of 1964, later amended by the Equal Employment Act of 1972.) Therefore, an employer can fire an employee who is not doing his job and can refuse to hire or fire anyone for any reason not prohibited by law. Other reasons include the following: the employee not doing his job, business being slow, the employer not liking the employee, or the employer's nephew needing a job. For whatever reason, an employee in a small company where the employer and employee work in close contact with each other is not as likely to question the reasons for being fired. Most of the time, the fired employee knows and accepts the firing and refrains from outright protest, hoping to at least get a letter of reference for his next job.

In larger corporations, employees are often fired through a separate personnel department. The large companies have their own attorneys who are well aware of the legal implications in terminating an employee. Yet it is surprising to learn that many large corporations will bend over backwards or go to extremes to avoid firing an employee. This is accomplished through counseling sessions between supervisors and employees or between a representative of the personnel department and the employee. It is also done through lateral moves, transferring the employee somewhere else in the organization. These companies do so (they say) because they do not want a reputation as a firm that easily fires its people, nor does it want to give its employees a reason for wanting a union.

EEOC

For detailed information and procedures concerning the Equal Employment Opportunity Commission and hiring/firing policy issues, refer to the EEOC's *Procedures Manual.* Below is a list of some important relevant concerns.

EEOC investigations cover firms employing fifteen or more employees. The EEOC gets involved only when disputes between employees and management involve matters of discrimination, including race, color, religion, sex (including sexual harassment), age, and national origin. Of these, the highest increase with a national impact has occurred with regard to sex discrimination, and 25 percent of these cases come under charges of "sexual harassment." At the EEOC, the administrative process takes place in the following way:

1. *Pre-charge filing state.* An employee who feels he has been discriminated against by a company because of race, color, religion, sex, or national origin goes to the EEOC and files a complaint against the company. He visits a pre-charge counselor or intake officer with the complaint. The burden of proof on the grievant is minimal at this stage. He must explain why he feels he has a complaint, and he must identify the parties involved. This minimal burden of proof does not hold in "failure to hire" cases because the complainant/grievant would not be in a position to supply the "who, why" facts.

For example, at quitting time, 500 employees pass through the company gate to go home; 499 are males, and only one is female. A female might be able to prove discrimination based on "failure to hire" if she applied for an advertised job and was not talked to or hired although she was otherwise qualified.

2. *Investigative hearing.* The "no-fault" stage. At this stage the EEOC is willing to approve anything both parties will agree to. The EEOC acts as mediator, or third party. Both parties attend the hearing. Attorneys may be present, but only as counselors; they cannot question the other party. Both parties are *invited* to resolve problems through a "no-fault" settlement arrangement. If agreement/resolution is reached, meaning a solution is acceptable to both parties, the matter is *settled.*

The EEOC would like all cases settled at this point, since taking the process further can be very costly to either (or both) management and employees—in time and money. In matters involving unions, it is often necessary for the EEOC to make both parties stay in the same room and continue to talk, rather than to adjourn. The EEOC mediator has the power to adjourn or not adjourn. If the matter is not settled, the next step must be taken.

3. *Full investigative hearing.* Involving facilitators/investigators. A full investigation is made as to the merits of a complaint. At this point, the situation no longer can come under "no-fault" settlement. The grievant/complainant continues with this grievance/complaint. At this point the federal government is involved and it is the EEOC's responsibility to see that relief is "proper and full" within the law.

Back pay may be awarded to an entire "affected class" and may extend up to two years prior to the date the discrimination charge is filed. Lengthy processes of investigation, attempted conciliation, and legal action often add years to the period involved, at great expense to the employer. It is the *consequence* of employment practices, *not* the *intent,* that determines whether there is discrimination requiring remedial action.

The EEOC will not approve a settlement unless it covers *full relief* and a motion is made for a *conciliation* process. Full relief includes the following:

- Reinstatement of employee to position.
- Full back pay.
- Restoration of lost benefits, which includes restoration of medical benefits the employee might have been entitled to through group insurance or company insurance benefits had he remained employed.

Steps 1–3 are called the "administrative process."

If the EEOC has given its "piece of paper" backing up an employee, the employee has won half the battle. Therefore, much weight is given to the EEOC's position on the case. It must be noted that the EEOC has no *power* or *authority* to issue a desist order: They are merely investigators and cannot make findings of discrimination on their own. They can only make recommendations.

In the judicial process in federal district court, the EEOC has no control over time or the numbers of court cases or judges. Companies involved in EEOC court cases should keep in mind that for each additional day required to reach a settlement or end of a case, the company pays that much more if the decision by the court is found to be against the company.

Class Action Suits

There is a difference between one individual filing a complaint against a company and several persons filing a complaint under a "class action suit." In a one-to-one situation, an attempt is made to establish or gather evidence to establish a prima facie case—by having enough evidence to establish a "reasonable cause" decision and *only* within range of a particular issue.

In a class action challenge, the administrative process is longer. The EEOC looks at how employment practices affect *everyone*. The EEOC looks at

- Discharge policies.
- Hiring policies.
- Promotion policies.
- Benefits policies.

Actions to eliminate class-wide discrimination must apply to all members of the "affected class." Any employment pracice—however neutral in intent and however impartially administered—that has a *disparate effect* on members of a "protected class" (those groups specified by law) or that *perpetuates the effect* of prior discrimination practices, constitutes unlawful discrimination, unless it can be proven that such policy is compelled by a realistic business necessity.

To justify any practice or policy that has a disparate effect on groups protected by law, an employer must present or demonstrate a compelling business necessity and show that no alternative nondiscriminatory practice can achieve the required purposes. A highly disproportionate representation of minorities or females in any job classification—in relation to their presence in the population or work force—also constitutes strong statistical evidence of discriminatory practices. The burden of proof is on the employer to show that the statistics are not the result of overt or institutional discrimination. "Business necessity," as interpreted by the courts, requires overriding evidence that a discriminatory practice is *essential* to safe and efficient operation of the business or demonstration of extreme adverse financial impact.

Additional Legal Information on EEOC

1. *Business need* as a defense is not a good argument for a discrimination complaint. For example, consider a restaurant in Georgia: management says he has nothing against blacks, but if he hired them he would have no customers and would go out of business. This is considered discrimination. But in border areas of the United States and Mexico or Canada, where management will not hire monolingual persons for jobs involving face-to-face, ear-to-ear contact, there would be no discrimination. The key to this issue is that the public would not benefit if monolingual persons were hired.

2. *"Authenticity,"* especially with regard to theatrical or acting professions, can be used as a basis for hiring or firing. There is no discrimination in a job advertised for a "beautiful woman" to play Juliet in *Romeo and Juliet*.

3. *The minimum wage statute.* There can be differences among companies in payment of wages over minimum wage scales. For example, one company can pay six dollars an hour to a machinist while another company can pay eight dollars an hour to a machinist. But within an individual company, *all* machinists must be paid the same amount per hour for the same work. In light of this, a recent Supreme Court decision allows women to sue in pay disputes where they do jobs unequal to male jobs, but the decision stopped short of advocating equal pay for jobs of "comparable worth."

4. *"Bonafide occupational qualifications"* (BFOQ) for jobs that require race, sex, or age as part of the qualifications are *rare*. The burden of proof that a particular descriptive characteristic is a BFOQ rests solely on the employer.

AFFIRMATIVE ACTION AND HIRING

There has been a profound impact of the EEOC and Affirmative Action on company personnel departments, their policies, their organization, and their day-to-day activities with regard to hiring and firing personnel.

Equal employment opportunity is the right of all persons to work and to advance on the basis of merit, ability and potential. State fair-employment laws and presidential orders in the 1940s and 1950s proved insufficient, and Congress passed federal legal enforcement for equal employment in the Civil Rights Act of 1964 and the additional strengthening amendments in 1972.

Title VII of the Civil Rights Act Prohibits discrimination because of race, color, religion, sex, or national origin in all employment practices, including hiring, firing, promotion, compensation and other terms, privileges, and conditions of employment. The courts prohibit "passive" as well as "active" discrimination. The EEOC was created to administer Title VII and to assure equal treatment for all in employment.

The courts, in interpreting the equal employment law, have clearly recognized the existence of "systematic" discrimination and the need to eliminate it through specific remedial actions. Title VII provides that when a court finds employment discrimination, it may "order such affirmative action as may be appropriate" to eliminate it. Where courts have found that the *effects* of employment practices—regardless of intent—discriminate against a group protected by law, they have ordered specific affirmative actions to eliminate present and future discrimination and to provide equitable remedies for consequences of past discrimination.

Executive Order 11246 (as amended by Executive Order 11375) requires all major nonconstruction contractors and subcontractors to conduct their own self-analysis to determine if their employment system has discriminatory effects and to take appropriate remedial affirmative action, without need of any legal proceedings. The order requires large contractors to implement written Affirmative Action plans, and regulations spell out detailed requirements for such plans.

Title VII does not explicitly require affirmative action. However, when there is a finding of discrimination through compliance investigation or through company self-audit, the EEOC is guided by remedies and requirements outlined by the federal courts.

The March 1972 amendment to Title VII gave the EEOC direct access to the courts, resulting in increased legal actions, but more recently several attempts have been made to reduce job discrimination rules for companies with federal contracts. Under fire is Executive Order 11246, which bars employment discrimination by federal contractors and aims to increase employment for women and minorities. Easing the rules would cut by two-thirds the number of companies covered by federal requirements. As of this writing, Executive Order 11246 is still effective.

SUMMARY
OF LAW AND ORDERS

Below is a summary of the major federal laws and administrative law orders that have an impact on firing.

The Equal Pay Act of 1963(22) requires all employers subject to the Fair Labor Standards Act (FLSA) to provide equal pay for men and women performing similar work. In 1972, coverage of this act was extended beyond employees covered by FLSA to an estimated fifteen million additional executive, administrative, and professional employees (including academic, administrative personnel, and teachers in elementary and secondary schools) and to outside sales people (through Title IX of the Education Amendments Act of 1972).

Title VII of the Civil Rights Act of 1964 (as amended by the Equal Employment Opportunity Act of 1972(20)–Title VII) prohibits discrimination because of race, color, religion, sex, or national origin, in any term, condition, or privilege of employment. The Equal Employment Opportunity Act of 1972 greatly strengthened the powers and expanded the jurisdiction of the EEOC in enforcement of this law. As amended, Title VII covers the following:

- All private employers of fifteen or more persons.
- All educational institutions, public and private.
- State and local governments.
- Public and private employment agencies.
- Labor unions with fifteen or more members.
- Joint labor-management committees for apprenticeship and training.

The Age Discrimination in Employment Act of 1967(23) prohibits employers of twenty-five or more persons from discriminating against persons between forty and sixty-five in any area of employment because of age.

Revised Order No. 4 (1970): Affirmative Action Programs are issued by the Office of Federal Contract Compliance, U.S. Department of Labor. These requirements include identifying areas of minority and female "underutilization," numerical hiring and promotion goals, and other actions to increase minority and female employment in job classifications where they are currently underutilized. (Order No. 4 is part of Executive Order 11246, amended by Executive Order 11375(21).

Executive Order 11246 was issued in 1965. It requires Affirmative Action Programs by all federal contractors and subcontractors and requires that firms with contracts over $50,000 and fifty or more employees *develop and implement* written programs, which are monitored by an assigned Federal Compliance Agency.

Other Laws
- *Executive Order 11141* affects ages between forty and seventy as a protected class.
- *Rehabilitation Act of 1973* affects, protects the handicapped.
- *National Labor Relations Act* provides there be no discrimination by unions.
- The *Civil Rights Acts of 1866 and 1870* and the *Equal Protection Clause of the Fourteenth Amendment.*
- The *Civil Rights Act of 1968.*

HOW TO AVOID
LEGAL DIFFICULTIES

Managers and legal counsels are unanimous in their advice when it comes to firing: use *common sense.* When documenting, make sure it is done evenly, fairly, impartially, and applies to *all.* Be sure that company policy with regard to discipline and firing includes *written* procedures that are disseminated throughout the company, especially within management. During the first few days after a new managerial-level employee is hired, she or he should be given a copy of procedures and should be required to *read* and *sign* them.

A common sense company policy on discipline and firing is applied evenly and fairly and includes the following:

1. A written job description on all employees.
2. Knowledge of what is expected of you and of each employee.
3. Evaluation of employees on a regular basis.

Also, a company should have the following in each employee's file:

1. Written employment rules. These should be given to each employee, and the employee should be required to read and sign them.
2. An employment application with a statement that if the application is falsely filled out, the employee could be discharged. This is one area where most companies fail.
3. For salaried employees—especially supervisors and middle-level managers—an employment contract giving details of the employer's right to fire, the employee's right to quit, and a "protection" clause for the company which includes a noncompetitive clause. Nonexistent a few years ago, employment contracts are rapidly becoming the norm for management.

A common reason why companies fail to take these simple steps is the time and money involved, especially for documentation. Experience and caseloads show that there is a high frequency of labor/management suits during periods of high unemployment. During periods of low unemployment, fired employees find it easy to get another job. The fired employee will not think about a lawsuit.

When confronting an employee with a firing message, be very careful. Choose your words well. Make special effort not to malign the character of the fired employee. Do not accuse him unless you know you can back it up!

Communicate to everyone at every level what is expected. Write it and make sure it is read and signed—especially among professional employees and upper-level management. At this level, employees are intelligent and experienced enough to know when they are not performing, but the problem is usually lack of communication between levels. It is easier to motivate an engineer (already in a professional field) than it is to motivate an unskilled factory worker.

Enforce policies fairly, consistently, evenly, *but with room for judgment* with regard to each situation. Ask what is involved. Ask for the record of the employee. Has he been given a chance to improve? What were the circumstances? "Judgment" in this instance should be included because it is very difficult to formulate and write only one inclusive policy to fit all situations that never happen exactly the same way more than once.

One authority stated that if more companies would approach firing decisions as though the company had a union, more of the people in management would *have* to know about specific laws and practices that apply to all companies and employees. In her view, documentation should be fair and should include both "good" and "bad" information. By adopting a systematic and even approach, we not only avoid labor disputes, but in the long run, we will find our jobs somewhat easier to perform. Documentation requires time and money, but labor suits involve much, much more.

CONCLUSION

We have discussed many circumstances that call for the dismissal of an employee. In no case should dismissal be undertaken without careful investigation and a weighing of the facts for that particular personnel case. All managers must be aware of their legal obligations and requirements. Management should be familiar with the background, progress, and implications of the law in order to maintain awareness of how the laws work at both the individual and institutional levels.

The National Labor Relations (Wagner) Act provides for priority treatment of cases involving certain alleged unfair labor practices, but it does not include those in which an employee has been fired. Section 10(L) may be amended to include cases in which an employee has been fired during a union representation election, or after a union has been designated to represent the employees, but before a collective bargaining agreement has been negotiated. As amended, Section 10(L) of the Wagner Act would require that the NLRB give precedence in the disposition of these cases, as well as others contained in Section 10(L).

Labor laws, presidential orders, and certain agency regulations are constantly changing, hopefully to benefit the employee-employer relationship. It is up to management to make sure that there is a fair and open approach toward labor disputes. With careful preparation, sound legal counsel, and common sense management, you can avoid those disputes that eventually end up being settled by the judicial system.

IV
CONCLUSION

14

Managerial Stress: Hiring and Firing Problems

Every survey of managers cites "firing employees" as a major cause of job-related stress.[1] Hiring people is not far behind, since the pressure is on every manager to make the best decision when hiring. Indeed, many a manager's performance is primarily judged by the quality of the people she hires. And who can dispute the stomach-churning effects of having to daily manage a situation where there is problem employee behavior upsetting the organization?

All the management problems we have discussed so far bring stress with them. Effectively managing these problems using the techniques outlined in the preceding chapters is a big step in the direction of keeping harmful stress within manageable limits. Still, stress is a major killer and disabler of managers today, and all signs point to it remaining a major threat for managers in the future.

What can managers do to remove some of the effects of stress caused by problem employees? What strategies can managers take to head off stress before it becomes a contributor to our managerial problems?

WHAT IS STRESS?

According to experts, stress is the body's response to any demand placed on it, pleasant or unpleasant. The actual amount of stress that is damaging to any one individual will vary widely, but each of us has a limited tolerance for stress. Failing to recognize that limit and failing to manage to keep stress within that limit can have serious consequences. Stress is a natural outcome of a variety of pressures and forces that come together in an individual's personal or professional life. It results from too much to be done, too little time in which to do it, too many decisions to be made, and too many people demanding too much from those decisions and those who make them. It comes from the actual physical nature of some task demands, and it comes also from the crush of mental and emotional demands that are placed on us—such as hiring new employees, managing problem employees, and firing unproductive or unneeded employees.

What do you know about heart attacks? What is the primary cause of such attacks?

- High blood pressure?
- High cholesterol?
- Smoking?
- Poor exercise habits?

According to the director of the Cardiovascular Center at the University of Nebraska, more than 50 percent of all heart attacks they see are not caused primarily by these commonly identified causes. They are caused by *stress*.

A Contradiction

The foregoing appears to be something of a contradiction. On one hand, we are suggesting that stress is bad—leading to strokes, heart attacks, and other negative health consequences. On the other hand, we suggest that stress also results from pleasant or positive situations. We might go further still and suggest that some stress is desirable and necessary in each of our lives. Think about the positive role of stress in your personal and professional life.

- A deadline may cause you to write a better report, complete a better project, or prepare a better presentation for the annual meeting.
- A sweaty-palm/dry-throat/tight-stomach response to stress before a speech may result in you giving a better speech.
- A stress-laden anticipation of an anniversary party, birthday celebration, or night on the town may add to the pleasure you derive from experiencing the event.
- Tension you feel right before participating in an athletic contest may result in better performance.
- The stress pressure that results in the so-called second effort may actually result in turning a losing contestant into a winner.

In each of these situations, stress and the body's response to stress are absolutely necessary for success. Many managers feel that if there is not enough stress to keep them (and their staffs) productive, they must introduce some stress just to keep things happening.

In our primitive ancestors, danger caused what experts called the fight-or-flight syndrome. When faced with danger, the body's natural defenses begin to operate. The heart begins to pump faster, the blood circulates, and breathing becomes heavier (reactions we now feel in an exciting football game or before going into a board meeting). In early humans, these bodily reactions were necessary to make the individual ready for physical reaction to danger.

WAYS TO COPE WITH STRESS

Today, our bodies still react in the same way to threats or danger, but we're no longer permitted to respond in the physical and aggressive way the cave man did. Instead, society has conditioned us to suppress our natural instincts for physical reaction, and the once-productive danger reactions of the body can now turn against us. We see the result in an increase in chronic fatigue, headaches, impaired vision and hearing, backaches, and often a total breakdown of the individual.

Many executives respond to the pressures of their jobs by putting the job ahead of their personal lives. This, say experts, is a prime cause of distress and can lead to serious personal consequences. Even if the executive is able to avoid personal problems resulting from stress, there is often an overflow of stress on the executive's staff.

Art Holst, the National Football League referee, when asked if Vince Lombardi had ulcers, is fond of replying, "No, but he was a carrier." So, too, are many managers and executives. Thus, developing a strategy for reducing stress can have organizational as well as personal benefits. The subject of stress and stress management is one filled with contradictions. In order to put stress in its proper perspective, let's examine the negative aspects and dimensions of stress.

Burnout

A relatively new dimension to the subject of stress is executive, managerial, or professional burnout. The public's awareness of burnout began with stories about the problems of teachers in inner-city schools and of air traffic controllers. In each of these professions, individuals were overloading, showing clear symptoms of stress and failure to perform at a fairly young age and with only a few short years on the job. This burnout, most of us thought, was due to the obvious and constant demands of these high-pressure careers. Such burnout, we may also have felt, would never be a problem for managers, college professors, or other professionals who experience only "moderate" and "infrequent" stress. Today, a quick review of journal and magazine articles about persons in all areas of endeavor will show the evidence: burnout is a problem of universal concern. In some groups, it is epidemic. Nurses, military officers, public managers, corporate executives, sports coaches, entertainers, even farmers, recreation directors, and persons of the clergy are not immune. Most managers know friends, colleagues, or co-workers who have experienced some of the symptoms of burnout. If you were not aware of it before, you should be now; stress and its damaging consequences has a firm hold on today's manager.

Burnout can occur in several forms. In some cases, only one or two isolated individuals are affected. In other cases, whole departments or groups within an organization are affected. In either from, burnout has a number of symptoms and "signals." Among them, are the following:

- A "burned-out" person's work efficiency declines markedly, as does his general initiative and work interest.
- A person refuses to cooperate with others, and he cites dissatisfaction with his jobs as the main reason.
- A person behaves negatively toward his work group or toward the entire organization and profession. In conversation, he depreciates his profession or organization, and he attempts to portray his personal efforts and contributions as unappreciated or unnoticed.
- As a group, people who have burnout have markedly higher turnover and absenteeism than those not burned out.
- A person blames scapegoats—superiors, politicians, spouses, even vague others such as "they"—for his own errors and failures.
- A person becomes disoriented and may actually show signs of mental or physical breakdown during rush periods or during other occurreances of outside caused stress.
- In career terms, a person begins to consider alternative occupations, even though he may not admit (even to himself) that he is doing so.

Burnout is one of the extreme consequences of job-induced stress. The other physical and emotional consequences of stress are better known. Many of these consequences can be avoided or minimized if executives follow a few simple approaches to stress, beginning with some self-analysis.

Are You a Victim of Stress?

No two individuals are alike in responding to the damaging side of stress. You are a prime candidate for stress-induced consequences if too many of the following traits or attitudes are currently true about you.

1. Do you have a constant almost overwhelming sense of the passage of time? Are you aware of your aging? Do you feel you don't have "enough time" left in your life?
2. Do you fail to delegate? Are you unwilling to let go of a project when you've finished with it? Do you feel subordinates are not quite up to handling things without your immediate supervision?
3. Do you voluntarily give up, pass by, or conveniently forget to take vacations? Do you take work with you when you do vacation? Do you feel guilty when that work does not get done?
4. Do you feel that your work is the only important thing in your life? Do you find it difficult to leave work? Do you ignore all facets of your life except work? (This is the classic "workaholic," a problem in part because she is steadily working toward a burnout or stress-induced breakdown. A problem too, because she is so productive. How can any

manager, faced with a subordinate with workaholic tendencies, tell that person to slow down? Until it's too late, of course.)

5. Do you take on too many projects, often with conflicting or overlapping deadlines? Do you find it difficult saying no when asked to do a favor or "just one more?" Do you succumb to flattery that leads you to taking on too much?

6. Do you talk fast and think fast and expect others to do likewise? Do you feel normal conversation, even social conversations, proceed at a too slow a pace? Do you "help" people by finishing their sentences for them?

7. Do you have a compulsive need for affirmation, to be told you're doing a good job? Do you need to be told you're great at golf, tennis, sex, gardening, or whatever? Is that need for affirmation coupled with a continuing drive to advance, to achieve, to win in all competitive situations?

8. Do you speak in bursts? Do you have explosive speech and behavior patterns?

9. Do you generally behave in a humorless manner? Do you find it difficult to laugh? Do you think that jokes, office high jinks, and general socializing are immature, irrelevant, and a waste of time?

10. Do you have a melancholy feeling of disappointment or regret? Do you feel that life holds few pleasures? Do you feel that past pleasures in activities or relationships will never again happen to you?

This portrait of the stress victim is not very pretty. Because it is not complimentary, there's a possibility that many stress-affected persons will ignore their own peril. They may choose to overlook the accuracy of this portrait, choosing instead to attribute stress and stress consequences to others. The "it-doesn't-apply-to-me" syndrome is a common one. Self-analysis is difficult. It is also very rewarding, and it is the first critical step in keeping stress under control.

Socrates suggested that self-analysis is the beginning of real wisdom. When his enemies accused him of thinking himself superior to others, he replied, "if this is so, I am superior only in self-awareness." He was able to listen to his inner voice and respond to its commands. He obeyed the divine command of the ancients, the command to "know thyself." Such a command is also a must for today's executive.

HANDLING DAMAGING STRESS

There are many ways to deal with stress. Perhaps the simplest is to avoid those situations where stress is caused or created. Although this is a foolproof way of dealing with stress, it's not very practical. Few of us can simply drop out of our society and move to a place where stress doesn't exist. Therefore, we must realistically face up to the situation. Without prescribing any specific solution for the problems of stress, here are several approaches that managers, in increasing numbers, are using.

Most authorities agree that there are two general categories of strategies for handling the damaging stresses in our personal and professional lives. These strategies are physical and sociopsychological.

Socio-Psychological Strategies

All of the strategies in this category involve the same advice: change your attitude about how you handle life events. Since this is a vague strategy to implement, let's take a closer look at how to change these attitudes for the better.

The word stress, as it relates to human behavior in response to pressure, is generally credited to Dr. Hans Seyle. Dr. Seyle is a medical doctor who is presently the director of the Institute for Stress Research in Montreal. His research and that of his colleagues has contributed much to our understanding of stress and how it can be combated.

Dr. Seyle suggests a sort of "recipe" or program that each of us can follow to minimize the damaging consequences of stress. Each of his steps can be applied independently, and each is the essence of simplicity and common sense. Together, this recipe is an excellent approach for management people interested in taking hold of stress before it takes hold of them.

1. *Learn about your stress factors.* This is largely a continuation of self-analysis. Look at your life on the job or off and try to develop a list of things that cause stress. Be sure to list both pleasant *and* unpleasant causes. Focus on those of a recurring nature, those that can be predicted. For example, we all experience stress (pleasant and unpleasant) during Christmas, New Year's, and other holidays, even if these events have religious significance for us. The same goes for anniversaries (weddings, divorces, or birthdays). Promotions, transfers, deadlines, workloads, job changes, organization growth, and moving to new facilities all carry stress potential. Make your list detailed, and make it inclusive.

Examine periods in your recent life when you feel you operated well, without any apparent negative consequences from stress. Examine those periods when there was too much stress and also those periods when there was too little stress. Your objective in the first part of Seyle's recipe is to develop a gauge of stress in your life. This will become a guide, a bench mark that helps indicate how much stress is good for you—and how much is harmful.

2. *Set your goals—and be sure they're yours.* Goal setting is a time-honored approach to every kind of problem solving. We begin every aspect of effective management with some statement of goals, and stress management is no exception.

However, Dr. Seyle's research suggests that too often the goals we say we're working toward are not really the goals we want to reach *for ourselves.* In short, we espouse goals espoused on us by others. We may not even recognize that those goals have actually been imposed on us by others. Those doing the imposing may not even be aware that they have done so, but the result is just as damaging in stress terms.

Why do you want to succeed? Is success (measured in money, power, position, satisfaction) something you really want, or have others (parents, friends, spouses, children, society) imposed the goals of "success" on you? How about your other goals—self or otherwise imposed?

Notice that no value judgment is being placed on any goal. The "stress test" for a goal is the way we come to value that goal. When a goal is imposed on us by others, there is going to be a constant internal struggle taking place in the individual. He may not realize that the struggle is taking place, just as he may not realize that there are imposed goals conflicting with "real" or "for me" goals. But the result is the same—more stress.

Consider the plight of the perpetual dieter. This person is constantly told that "thin is in," that "you can't be too rich or too skinny," that real success in management, like success in love, athletics, or politics, goes to the slim and trim. Losing weight becomes an obsession. Every conversation contains a gem such as, "I'm really going to get off these extra pounds right after the holidays" (or after the audit, or before vacation, or whatever).

Sit with the dieter for a family meal just as the apple pie dessert is being served, watch the agony, and remember the decision process. "Do I or don't I eat that pie?" If the decision is "I'll eat the pie, but I won't enjoy it, and I'll pay it back tomorrow," it's a fair assumption that you're watching a person in a goal conflict. The "do it but feel the need to profess guilt" approach is laden with stress. The individual's real goal may be to enjoy life, but to enjoy life and be overweight is socially unacceptable. The net result is a life of anxiety, guilt, Jekyl-versus-Hyde behavior (starve in public, overeat in private), and stress.

Subjects such as dieting, smoking, drinking, sex, church attendance, civic responsibility, and family duties are constant sources of conflicting goal-related stress. So too are such areas as organization, upward mobility, status seeking, and financial success.

As you list and examine your goals, try to sort out those that are really your own from those that you want to reach but are being imposed by others. The commitments you make to your own goals should take precedence over those that are imposed, even though many of those imposed goals are clearly beneficial to you and are worthwhile in their own right. The priorities you thus establish can help reduce some of the stress that affects your overall performance. Removing or reducing that stress can actually give you more time and energy to work on those goals imposed by others that do not seriously conflict with your real goals.

3.   *Adopt a new code of behavior.* Ultimately, controlling stress means taking control of our behavior. The way you handle conflicts and the way you communicate with others will directly affect your ability to manage stress. Following are some specific suggestions for behavior changes:

Plan your time. When the time begins to slip away, pressures begin to mount. By scheduling your time to accomplish the things that are important to you, you'll free up plenty of time to devote to exercise, self-analysis, and development of relationships. Also, better time management will remove some of the self-imposed pressures on you that actually contribute to stress.

Manage conflicts. Some of us handle every conflict by trying to avoid it. We use the philosphy that "there's no problem so big or so complicated it can't be run away from." Others try to treat every conflict as a "win-lose" situation. They use every tactic and strategy available to defeat the other person or party. In the end, they wind up with a lot of disgruntled losers, each aching to exact some measure of revenge. Just keeping past and future adversaries off your back could be a full-time job.

For many of us, the best way to handle conflict is to strike a deal, to bargain and compromise in every situation. This approach results in many fine conflict solutions, but it may also lead to many uneasy feelings that we're obtaining workable rather than optimal solutions to our problems. Also, some conflicts simply don't lend themselves to compromise. The frustration that results from trying to compromise the uncompromisable can add additional stress to your life.

The optimizing approach to conflict management is to treat every conflict as part of an ongoing process. Thus, how you handle a given conflict will influence how future conflicts develop. For example, if you defeat the manager of a rival department in a dispute over allocation of resources, the victory may come back to haunt you in a future problem, when you need that manager's help. If you make a deal in the same conflict, the bad feelings that often result when we "settle for less than we deserved" can create future difficulties.

When faced with a conflict, on the job or off, keep both you and your opponent focusing on the problem rather than on the specific solutions you each want to see implemented. When you have hostile feelings about the other person, get them out in the open. This way, these feelings don't become "hidden agendas," fouling up the discussion of the problem and contributing to additional stress. Try to avoid placing blame for the conflict you are in and instead focus on the mutual benefits to be derived from an optimal solution.

Improve communication. Learn to listen better, and learn to express what is really on your mind. When listening, encourage the other person by thoughtful eye contact and an occasional head nod. Give other people a chance to say what is on their minds. When talking, be mindful of the body language you're using, and be careful to avoid saying one thing and doing the opposite. Actions speak louder than words, and we often confuse others and contribute to their stress and our own when we create such miscommunications.

Analyze your "transactions" with others. Transactional analysis, or TA, is also a stress-reducing strategy that is somewhat unconventional, at least among supervisors. Yet it too can provide some welcome relief from the pressures of stress around us.

Transactional analysis is a system for defining and analyzing what occurs between people when they attempt to communicate. It also involves other related theories of personality. In technical terms, a transaction is a single unit of social interaction in a chain of interactions.

TA emphasizes the importance of dealing with people on an honest, straightforward, responsible basis. According to TA proponents, we often avoid such dealings because of ego defenses and lack of trust in other people. Obviously, it is important for managers to develop trust, especially in building a team that contributes to the development of a motivating environment.

Many companies, including Sears Roebuck & Co., Associated Merchandising Corp., Bank of New York, Bank of America, 3M Co., Westinghouse, Honeywell, Metropolitan Life Insurance, TRW, Inc., and General Foods, are using TA for their supervisory and executive staffs.

There is no specific TA program. Rather, it is applied to supervisory problems in a consulting way, usually through some organized program. You can develop some insight into the TA philosophy by reading books on the subject. In particular, start with the pioneer work on TA, Eric Berne's *Games People Play*. Like the other strategies, the success or failure of applying TA in helping you to control and reduce stress in your life is directly related to the amount of interest and enthusiasm you develop for the approach.

Treat people as adults. (and expect) adult treatment in return. When we treat peers, subordinates, or members as children while we play the parent role, we usually create considerable stress for them. Of course, some people like to be treated as children, and with care, they should be treated in that way. For the majority of people, however, we work best when we can engage in adult relationships. The adult-adult approach, although it may take more time to maintain than the more controlling parent-child relationship, can have a significant impact on the stress in our lives and those with whom we work.

Reduce uncertainty. A serious cause of stress is uncertainty. When we're not sure about where we are going, stress develops and accentuates other problems and pressures. When dealing with subordinates, try to reassure them as much as possible about what changes are impending, and keep in mind that such reassurances can pay off in terms of better performance and better support for you. Keep people informed, since information is a good way to reduce uncertainty and the stress that comes with it. An organization that follows a policy of maintaining healthy communication from top to bottom keeps everyone operating at a low "uncertainty level" and considerably reduces stress.

4. *Develop confidence in your competence.* One of the most troubling sources of stress is the feeling of purposelessness that plagues many people. This feeling stems either from a lack of direction in their lives or from the notion that their skills, talents, and abilities are obsolete, or quickly becoming obsolete. Managerial obsolescence is as important and as real as an athlete getting past his prime or an engineer not keeping up with advancements. However, it is not as often recognized as a potential source of stress. To avoid this sort of creeping purposelessness that afflicts many of us, develop and maintain a sense of your own competence. This may mean continuing education, either through your professional organization or through local educational institutions. It may be done through continued updating of your professional skills. Self-confidence as a hedge against purposelessness can also be acquired by developing "fallback" positions and skills, so that your world does not solely depend on your present job or your immediately usable skills.

Some time ago, at a convention of credit union managers, two executives were discussing a third individual, who had retired. From their conversation, it was apparent that this individual was gravely ill, mentally and physically. Casually listening to the conversation, one might assume that their friend had been retired for some time. Later, in a private conversation with one of the executives, the full story came out. The manager had retired six months before. At the time of his retirement, he managed one of the largest credit unions in his region of the country. Through wise investment and careful living, he was now able to live very comfortably in South Florida. He had plenty of leisure time activities at his disposal. His marriage and family relationships were sound. Yet, despite all these advantages, this individual was close to death. The opinion of the man's doctors was that he was a victim of purposelessness. On the job all his life, he developed no hobbies, no emotional or physical outlets other than his work. When the work disappeared, purposelessness rushed in. He was suffering from an extreme case of the same stress consequences that threaten anyone who starts to become obsolete. Be developing a feeling of self-confidence, along with a healthy respect for the prospect of continued change, we can overcome some of the potential for stress.

Physical Strategies

In general, the best advice from all stress experts is exercise. Regular, moderate, but challenging exercise is an excellent way to relieve stress. Such exercise should be appropriate to an individual's age, physical condition, past athletic experience, and general circumstances. All but the simplest physical approaches to stress management should be undertaken under a doctor's supervision. Improved diet, a positive change in patterns of sleep, nonphysical recreation (such as reading), and family or social contact are also quite useful.

Following are some immediately usable physical approaches to managing stress.

ENERGY-RELEASE TECHNIQUES

Some executives use energy-releasing techniques such as beating a pillow or pounding their fist into an object, preferably one that's not too hard.

This is something like a child's tantrum and is an effective way to release tension. However, it can't be practiced on the job, or at least not in a place where others will see or hear you, without some unfortunate reactions. Yet experts do insist that much of the damage done by stress is caused when aggressive feelings are not vented.

Some stress counselors suggest that we remove pent-up

aggressions by screaming (privately, of course) or doing in a controlled manner those things that can relieve normal tensions.

A radio station in North Carolina recently conducted two contests for its listeners. The prize for the drawing was a chance to blow up a bridge or a large smokestack. Both were scheduled for demolition anyway. The station was simply giving two people the chance to vent their frustrations while possibly fulfilling their fantasies. The response to the station's contest was overwhelming, suggesting that there's more pent-up frustration around than we might have imagined.

This doesn't mean that managers should go around beating up their employees or smashing desks, machinery, or walls to relieve anxiety and tension. It does suggest that acceptable outlets for tension (such as exercise) should be developed as habits and maintained by regular practice.

THERAPEUTIC VALUE OF SPORTS

An energy-releasing technique that has many side benefits is involvement in sports and exercise. For example, two executives who work for large national trade associations play handball three times each week, an hour at a time. They not only release their aggressions on the rubber ball (which one of the pair says he thinks of as his board chairman), but they also benefit from the exercise.

Don't overdo the exercise, however, and be sure that you're in shape to do what you are demanding of your body. If you've spent ten years of your life "flying a desk," you can't expect to be able to play five sets of tennis or run a mile before breakfast without serious repercussions. Consult a doctor, and be sure that you are prepared for your exercise. Also, get into the exercise gradually, building up to the point where you can enjoy and profit from your energy-releasing sessions.

NUTRITION

The relationship between physical condition, mental capability, and personal nutrition has been well established by medical and behavioral research. Despite this, we've become a society of junk-food freaks. Watch what you eat, and study the relationship between performance and nutrition. It's a good hedge against going off the deep end, and it can be a helpful complement to your stress-reducing strategy.

BENEFITS OF MEDITATION

For many executives, meditation sounds too far-out for them to even consider. Yet meditation has become an accepted solution to many of the stress-related problems that plague association managers. Professional football quaterbacks, advertising executives, municipal court judges, and longshoremen are all numbered among the adherents of one form or another of meditation. In the words of one manager who uses meditation, it's "a way of overcoming nervous tension. It's a non-chemical tranquilizer that has no unpleasant side effects and costs really nothing to use."

There are several avenues to follow in meditation. Perhaps the best known form of meditation is TM, or transcendental meditation.

TM's proponents are followers of the Marharishi Mahesh Yogi, a bearded guru from India whose movement is responsible for training classes and seminars around the country. These centers have introduced approximately 700,000 Americans to the benefits of their particular brand of meditation. According to the TM approach, meditation practitioners sit still for twenty minutes each morning and evening, repeating silently their personal Sanskrit word, called a *mantra*. According to the TM people, this procedure can overcome the unfortunate effects of everything from high blood pressure to lack of energy to alcoholism.

Scientific studies performed by experts not affiliated with the TM movement report that meditation (although not necessarily the TM variety) is responsible for a lowering of blood pressure, heart stress, fatigue, and other stress-related ills.

TM has many followers among managers, and an increasing number of companies and associations are investigating TM programs for their employees and staff.

There are other approaches to meditation that can achieve results similar to TM without the trappings of ceremony and the mysticism that many associate with TM.

Meditation involves four steps, which all proponents seem to agree on. These steps are as follows:

1. *Have a quiet environment.* This is important whether you are involved in meditation or not. A quiet time for contemplation and personal reflection is important if you are going to be ready to meet the challenges of a hectic environment. This point is particularly important in planning and managing your time. Meditation, to achieve the desired results, is best practiced in quiet and seclusion.

2. *Have an object to dwell upon.* For TM practitioners, this is the mantra, a saying that has no specific meaning to the individual and that is repeated over and over again. The importance of this focal point is apparently great. Other meditation enthusiasts suggest that a person intent on meditation substitute in place of a personal mantra a short simple phrase, or counting, or even a short prayer from one's religious traditions.

The benefits of prayer (quite apart from their theological value) are not to be overlooked. The quiet and contemplative environment, coupled with a familiar yet meaningful litany, induces a response similar to that resulting from meditation. It's interesting that we sometimes think people in earlier times were unsophisticated, but their common-sense notion of talking with God is at the heart of meditation today. Thus, believer or not, the renewing effects of a prayer chant are obvious.

3. *Develop a passive attitude.* This is perhaps the most important factor in most meditation concepts. In order to properly meditate and receive the maximum benefit from doing so, you must take on a passive attitude. This can be induced by deep breathing and by consciously emptying your mind of all thoughts except the mantra, or dwelling object. Don't be disturbed if random thoughts stray in. Simply concentrate in a passive way on what you are saying and maintain the rhythm of the breathing. Eventually, and with practice, the passive attitude can be maintained for longer and longer periods of time, and real meditation can begin.

4. *Assume a comfortable position.* This can be sitting or lying down, but should be a position that causes no external reaction (such as a chair arm sticking into your ribs). Be careful, however, that your meditation position is not so comfortable that you fall asleep.

One final point if you are considering meditation: don't jump in without any direction or guidance. If you have serious problems, consult with your doctor before trying meditation. If you prefer more structure, perhaps the TM approach, or one similar, will be to your liking. Don't write off meditation as something for others. The many executives who have adoped meditation are not wasting their time, and perhaps there are values in it for you as well.

YOUR BODY'S INNER CLOCK

Although not specifically a method for reducing stress and maintaining health, biorhythms do offer other insights into our behavior, and such insights can have healthful side benefits.

A biorhythm is an inner clock that regulates our physical, emotional, and intellectual ups and downs. By plotting these biorhythms, we are able tc know when we are at peaks or lows in our physical, intellectual, or emotional cycles and when these cycles are in their critical stages. Apparently, a critical point in a cycle is a warning for particular caution. According to the proponents of biorhythms, plotting your cycles and their critical points can help guard against potential trouble.

Your biorhythm is based on your birth date and on the fact that the three cycles each have a precise length. One expert on biorhythms notes that there is roughly an 80 percent connection between commercial airliner crashes and the critical biorhythmic days of the pilots involved.

Plotting one's biorhythms can help in planning activities or in giving advance notice when certain kinds of activities should be avoided. If biorhythm seems to appeal to you, look into it further. If properly used, it can give you an important edge on planning and scheduling your activities.

VACATION

If it seems somehow out of place to mention vacation with the other lofty concepts and programs we've been discussing, it's only because too often we overlook one of the simplest ways to control stress. Many managers fail to take vacations. They prefer to remain on the job solving problems. They justify their foregone vacations with such statements as "They'll never solve the Randall problem without me" or "if I let that assistant of mine take over even for a week, the whole staff will be botched up good" or "I love my work—every day is a vacation for me."

What these managers fail to recognize is that the body needs time to relax and prepare for new challenges. If kept going at full power for a long time, the body eventually strains beyond the breaking point and cannot recover. If you have trouble falling asleep, or if you find that after two days of vacation you are ready to be back into harness, perhaps you are feeling the warning signals of this breaking point. Pushed too far, you don't recover as fast, and eventually, you don't recover at all.

One Midwest manager keeps close watch on the vacation time of all his subordinates. If a subordinate approaches the end of the year without taking the full vacation due, this manager temporarily fires the offending person. He requires the employee to stay off the job until after the new year. This manager realizes that his people are not giving their best, and they can't be pushed when necessary if they don't take care of themselves and recharge their mental and physical batteries regularly. His approach has an interesting side benefit for him and his organization.

"Now," he admits, "they watch my vacation schedule, and they fire *me* if I don't take all my vacation each year." What's fair for the employees is fair for the boss.

A natural outgrowth of managerial responsibility is that you receive personal rewards from doing your job. You have an opportunity to do something meaningful and to receive many benefits. However, such rewards and benefits are no substitute for vacations and off-the-job recharging. An adequate vacation spent in real relaxation must be included in any stress-management strategy.

CONCLUSION

All organizations should be run according to sound management principles and with careful attention to work problems and employee concerns. By turning those same common-sense approaches to the problems of stress, it is possible to bring stress under control.

The strategies discussed in this chapter for coping with stress are by no means comprehensive, but they do provide a background for your personal planning and thinking. Consider each of the strategies in both categories with an open mind.

As a manager, you have a responsibility to your organization and your staff that extends beyond providing competent management. You have a responsibility to be at your best. This means reducing stress whenever possible. In doing so, you'll be happier and more productive.

Appendix:
Writing
A Professional Resume

Increasing job mobility has forced many people to face the problem of preparing an effective personal resume.[1] If you are called upon to do so, there are a few key concepts to keep in mind.

Even if you are not looking for a new job and don't need a resume at the moment, it is handy for you as an executive to have a solid working knowledge of resumes, as the basis for judging such documents when they are presented to you by job seekers. They can also be used for judging the job seekers themselves.

A resume represents one of the most important forms of communication a person can devise for use in shaping his or her career.

It should be truthful, but it can present the truth in a creative and interesting fashion.

A resume is an individual's self-advertisement. As such, it should be prepared with as much thought and care as advertising agencies and manufacturers give to the advertising and marketing of their products.

It should reflect everything that the job seeker wishes to convey to the potential employer.

A person's background, experience, and ability make up the most important product he or she will ever sell. Yet, too often, a good product is disastrously undersold.

Tendency
Toward Sameness

It has often been the practice for people preparing resumes merely to find an example that has worked before and to change the information slightly. The problem with standard-form resumes is that they have a disturbing tendency toward sameness and an inflexibility that does not permit maximum exposure of the individual's salable qualities.

A prospective employer looks for a resume that indicates thought and creativity in its preparation. This in itself tells a great deal about the applicant.

Although a form resume should be avoided in favor of a tailored resume, there are standards that should be followed. The resume should be brief but complete. It is important not to omit essential information. A poor resume will be ignored or discarded by the person who received it.

Most prospective employers prefer a one- or two-page resume. A common rule is to prepare one additional page for each ten years of schooling and work experience.

The background, education, and experience of the individual will determine the order of facts in his resume. Only facts that are particularly relevant to a prospective job should be highlighted. Omit the others.

For example, a graduating college senior who is well trained but inexperienced in a particular line of work would emphasize educational background. An experienced executive would highlight her major occupational responsibilities.

Types of Resumes

A general resume is the most common form of resume. It shows no attempt to emphasize particular experiences of the writer. It provides a prospective employer with a summary of the individual's experience. It can be converted to a "mass employment campaign" used by many people on their first venture into finding a job. It is flexible and applicable to a variety of career positions.

Other types of resumes have evolved to focus on particular areas of an individual's background. The *functional resume* translates an individual's work experience into terms more understandable to an employer. It is, for example, useful for a person who finds it necessary to translate military skills into terms that will be understood by civilian employers.

The functional resume is also used for the individual who has a generalist background and experience in a variety of managerial problems. For this person, a single job description on a general resume provides little insight into his capabilities, and the functional resume is a means for expanding on these varied experiences.

There are scores of other resume forms, from extremely detailed to vaguely general. The choice of style and format must be made by the individual, based on what he wishes the resume to accomplish.

Self-Analysis

In preparing a resume, an individual should first look at her interests and the reasons behind these interests. It is important to identify interests and abilities, evaluate them honestly, and express them clearly. Business and government leaders continually voice concern over the number of people coming to them for all kinds of employment who have no idea of their abilities in the business world.

Career Objective

A statement of career or job objective depends on the purpose of the resume. If a resume is to be used for a broad-based sounding-out of the job market, it should contain a statement of a career objective, phrased in general terms, but carefully avoiding a wishy-washy image.

If the purpose of a resume is to apply for a specific position, a career objective statement should be specific, although care must be taken to keep the statement from being too specific, thereby reducing the effectiveness of the entire message.

Preparing the Resume

It is important to remember that a resume summarizes what the individual has to offer a prospective employer. The people who read resumes are busy, so a brief and well-designed document is vital.

FUNCTIONAL TERMS

It is wise to begin each statement on a resume with a past-tense verb form. For example, "directed and supervised applied research in personnel administration," or "administered customer service training program." First-person references are usually avoided, although the choice of first-person or third-person reference is optional. Most people have trouble describing themselves in first-person terms and prefer the more objective-sounding third person.

FEEL

The importance of tactile communication cannot be underestimated. In preparing a resume, always use good quality paper in the standard size. Old sizes are difficult to handle and file, and the combination of cheap paper and unusual size may cause the prospective employer to form unfavorable impressions. Soft, understated colors are also effective, and loud colors are not.

COPIES

If copies are made, be certain that the copy process allows for use of good paper and that the copies are clear and precise. If the copy gives the impression of a mass run, it will substantially reduce the impact of the resume's contact.

BLANK SPACE

Use of blank space on a resume is important. It should be arranged to highlight the sections of the resumé. Too much open space gives an excessively idealistic image to the reader, and too little space gives an overly intense picture, indicating a cluttered mind and often an insecure personality. Asymmetrical arrangements are sometimes effective if properly done. Poorly handled asymmetry gives the impression of shallowness and a concentrated but futile attempt to impress.

IDENTIFICATION

Your name should be placed in a prominent location, in capital letters, on or near the top center of each page. If your resume exceeds one page, but does not quite fill two full pages, it is wise to divide the information appropriately between the two pages. Although sloppy typing is unappealing, a clean, attractive, well-spaced resumé on good paper can help get information to the person who makes hiring decisions.

WHAT TO AVOID

Never send a carbon copy of a resume to a prospective employer. The same holds true for resumés that have erasures or unsightly smudges. In view of the critical mission of the resume, time spent in retyping and reworking is well spent.

Try to send a resume to an individual manager who will be hiring. If this is not possible, send it to a firm's personnel office.

Abbreviations should never be used. Anything important enough to be mentioned should be written out. Abbreviations give the impression of an attempt to cram information. An exception is the common abbreviation for degrees and licenses, to be used only when the prospective employer will understand the meaning of such abbreviations (for example, MBA, BS, PhD, CAP, CFA).

A resume should not go into great detail on jobs below an individual's top level of employment. Such detail, unless relevant to the position sought, tends to confuse what could otherwise be an effective presentation of experience.

Avoid including your salary requirements. Discussion of salary is best left for later correspondence or personal interviews, where all factors can be included in consideration of this most important subject.

WHAT THE RESUME SHOULD CONTAIN

Although resumes differ depending on background and experience, they all contain basic categories of information. These categories include the following:

Name, Address, and Telephone Number.   The name should appear at the top of each page in capital letters. On the first page, in a prominent location, should be home address and telephone number, including area code. The present job address and telephone number is optional.

Personal Data.   A summary of relevant personal data should appear either near the top of the first page, balanced with the address and telephone number, or at the bottom of the last page. Include height, weight, condition of health (indicate good or excellent: if neither of these adjectives describes your health, it would be wise to discuss physical condition as a separate section, indicating particular disabilities and the extent to which these disabilities would interfere with job performance, marital status (if married, indicate the number of children or dependents), and birth date. Since equal employment opportunity laws prohibit discrimination on most of these factors, any personal information you give is voluntary and optional. Many people in recent years have begun omitting this section from their resumes.

Education.   In the section on education, list each college or university attended and its location, dates of attendance, degrees, areas of specialization, and briefly mention any academic honors or scholarships. List schools in reverse order, beginning with the last school attended.

For a college graduate, it is not necessary to mention high school. As an individual moves away from his school years, the education section of his resumé becomes less of a factor in his employment. This can be reduced until it mentions only those institutions from which he received academic degrees.

Military Service.   For the individual with military service, this section of the resume should include the branch of the service and dates of active duty, rank upon discharge, and a brief description of responsibilities. Include a statement of any reserve obligation. An individual with extensive military experience should translate such experience into civilian terms and include the information in the experience section of the resume.

Literary Accomplishments.   In standard form, list the title, journal, date, and page number of any articles published.

Personal Interests and Activities.   Since employers are interested in well-rounded individuals, it is wise to list interests in literature, athletics, and activity clubs or organizations. Mention should be made of offices held in civic and social organizations. A brief list of hobbies is sometimes useful.

References.   There are two schools of thought on references. One holds that all references should be included on the resume, and the other contends that only a brief statement, "references available on request," is necessary. The decision rests on the degree of flexibility desired for the resume.

Availability.   A date should indicate when the individual can begin work. An availability date gives the prospective employer some idea of when he can plan to hire an individual. Availability should also indicate feeling toward travel and relocation. The simple statement, "travel and relocation unlimited," gives a carte blanche to the prospective employer, and restrictions in travel give the employer notice of individual's preferences.

THE DYNAMIC RESUME

Your resume should be revised continuously to reflect changes in education and experience.

Perhaps the greatest mistake an individual can make is to assume that, once a resume is typed and prepared, it needs no further changing. The result, in the long run, does more harm than good to the individual's chances for successful employment.

Be creative. Use imagination. Seek advice and guidance. The result will be an effective professional resume and a step in the right direction in a job-seeking strategy.

Notes

CHAPTER 1

1. This section is from the author's article "Self-Analysis: First Step in Effective Communication," *Credit Union Management*, November/December 1978, pp. 7–10. Copyright© 1978 by the Credit Union Executives Society. Used with permission.

CHAPTER 2

1. Robert Presthus, *The Organizational Society* (New York: Knopf, 1962), pp. 164-286.

2. Lawrence J. Peter, *The Peter Principle* (New York: Holt, Rinehart & Winston, Inc., 1968).

3. The balance of this chapter, including the test at the end of the chapter, is based on material from an article by Thomas M. Rohan, "Should a Worker's Personality Affect Your Managing?" *Industry Week*, May 5, 1975, pp. 28–38. Copyright© 1975, Penton/IPC, Inc. Used with permission. Table 1 and the employee personality types are based on the research of V. Flowers and C. Hughes, as reported in the article cited above.

CHAPTER 4

1. This chapter is based on an article by the author, William Mitchell, and Brian Hawkins, "Developing your Interviewing Skills, Parts 1 and 2" *Credit Union Management*, Part 1, September 1979, pp. 22–25; part 2, October 1979, pp. 19–23. Copyright© 1979 by the Credit Union Executives Society. Used with permission.

2. The section on Listening Habits is from the author's article "Listening Habits, Listening Skills," *The Deltasig*, November 1976, pp. 6–10. Copyright© 1976 by the International Fraternity of Delta Sigma Pi. Used with permission.

CHAPTER 5

1. Title VII, Equal Employment Opportunity, Civil Rights Act of 1964, as amended March 24, 1972.

2. Title VII, Civil Rights Act of 1964, Section 703(h), Interpretative Statement (860:14) Bureau of National Affairs, *Labor Relations Reporter, Fair Employment Practices Manual*, 401:5077.

CHAPTER 6

1. This chapter is from an article by Harry David, "The Art of Checking References," *Nation's Business*, June 1981, pp. 82–85. Reprinted by permission from *Nation's Business*, June 1981. Copyright 1981 by *Nation's Business*, Chamber of Commerce of the United States.

CHAPTER 7

1. Morris Massey, *The People Puzzle* (Reston, VA: Reston Publishing Co., 1979).

2. Morris Massey, *What You Are Is Where You Were When*, a film produced by Inter-Video, Ann Arbor, Michigan, 1977.

CHAPTER 8

1. This section is based on the author's article "Use the Spoken Word to Put Across Your Message." Reprinted with permission from the August 1978 issue of *Association*

Management. Copyright© 1978 by the American Society of Association Executives, pp. 71-78.

2. This section is based on the author's article "Getting Your Ideas Across Persuasively," *Journal of the American Health Care Association,* January, 1979, pp. 8–11. Copyright© 1979 by the American Health Care Association. Used with permission.

3. John Weisman, "TV Reporting and Hostages," *TV Guide,* August 26, 1978, p. 6.

CHAPTER 9

1. This chapter is based on an article by the author and Brian Hawkins, "Creative Conflict Management." Reprinted, by permission of the publisher, from *Supervisory Management,* November 1979, pp. 7–11. Copyright© 1979 by AMACOM, a division of American Management Associations. All rights reserved.

CHAPTER 10

1. This chapter is based on an article by the author and Brian Hawkins, "Performance Appraisal: Evaluation and Communication," *Industrial Management,* January–February 1978, pp. 13–17. Used with the permission of the editor.

2. Douglas McGregor, "An Uneasy Look at Performance Appraisal," *Harvard Business Review,* 35:90 (May–June 1957), p. 87.

CHAPTER 12

1. Jim Bouton, *Ball Four* (New York: Dell, 1970), p. 157.

CHAPTER 14

1. This chapter is based on two articles by the author: "Physical Strategies for Coping with Stress." Reprinted with permission from the November 1976 issue of *Association Management,* pp. 46–49. Copyright© 1976 by the American Society of Association Executives. "Managing Managerial Stress," *Credit Union Management,* June 1980, pp. 10–17. Copyright© 1980 by the Credit Union Executives Society. Both articles are used with permission.

APPENDIX

1. This appendix is based on the author's article "The Importance of a Resume in Shaping Your Career" Reprinted with permission from the June 1973 issue of *Association Management,* pp.90–95. Copyright© 1973 by the American Society of Association Executives.

Index